A SPACE

BETWEEN

A SPACE

BETWEEN

A Journey of the Spirit

Ardeth De Vries

River Sanctuary
PUBLISHING
Felton, California

A Space Between: A Journey of the Spirit
Copyright © 2010 by Ardeth DeVries

Cover design by Ardeth De Vries based on original art by Ellaine Shannon.
Illustrations by Ellaine Shannon.

Interior design by DreamWriter (*www.dreamwriterservices.com*)

ISBN 978-0-9841140-2-3
Printed in the United States of America

To order additional copies please visit:
www.riversanctuarypublishing.com

River Sanctuary Publishing
P.O. Box 1561
Felton, California 95018
www.riversanctuarypublishing.com
Dedicated to the spiritual awakening of the New Earth

For Clarence and Ellaine with
love and thanks for the lessons

♥

ACKNOWLEDGEMENTS

Those of us who put thoughts down on paper for others to read don't live in a vacuum, and the people who read our words before they appear in book form deserve thanks for their contributions to the creative process. A special thank you to Marcy Bahr for her editing, insights and enthusiasm about the book and to Bruce Kint for his consistent support and feedback.

Thank you also to Annie Elizabeth and David at River Sanctuary Publishing for their love, creative energy, and for helping me give birth to this book. Your ideas, support, and connection to my words are very much appreciated.

And then there's Ellaine Shannon, my partner in this life for 40 years. (You'll meet her as Ho Yung in the book.) Ellaine has read every word of *A Space Between* in its various incarnations, and many years ago she drew the beautiful illustrations you'll see in the book. Even though she isn't physically present in this life any longer, Ellaine's energy still guides me as I continue my journey.

Finally, and most importantly, there's Clarence. Thank you, my friend, for being such a wonderful teacher, and for being the inspiration for this book. I miss our talks, but I know you're always with me, and I look forward to seeing you again in that space between. For now...just keep talking; sometimes I hear you.

A SPACE BETWEEN

THE OFFICE

THE LANE

THE AMUSEMENT PARK

EPILOGUE

Author's Note

Teachers (that's me sometimes) can often be a little over the top when they present lessons to be learned. But, sometimes a good story says it all, and no explanation is necessary other than a bit of instruction to think about the "moral" of the story. So, with the hope that the book you're about to read will offer lessons for your consideration, I'll resist the temptation to tell you what I'd like you to learn from this book. What you learn, if anything, is up to you.

Most of you will see this book as a fictional story, and that's fine with me. I don't actually think this book is fiction, but, hey, that's just my take on it. You get to read it in any way that works for you; I'm just the storyteller.

Imagine that you're in that space between lives, ready to experience a visit to Earth, or perhaps somewhere else. That's where I am in this book, and I'd like you to join me as I meet with my travel agent in his office. After our meeting we'll take a walk and meet some fascinating people and animals who will offer a variety of metaphorical lessons for us to consider. Once our journey down the lane is complete we'll end up at an amusement park where you can visit various attractions with me. Eventually I'll leave you as I travel down The Chute to be born here on Earth.

That's it. That's the plot of this book. Pretty simple, isn't it? But...maybe there's more to it than that. Could be, but I'll let you decide. Please join me.

Ardeth De Vries   January 2010

THE OFFICE

Who's Who

When we're in that space between, time and
distance don't exist.

I can't see him, but I know he's here.

Cigar smoke swirls around and above the mountain of papers growing from his desk, and the air is thick with a gray haze that smells of rum and rich Turkish tobacco. His favorite blend. Every so often a new puff of smoke launches itself from behind the paper mountain, challenging the lingering wisps that coat everything in the room.

Once, another moment ago, he'd asked me to purchase a box of his special cigars from a shop in London. I was in California at the time, which meant that little shopping trip would have involved physically traveling to a different continent while time traveling two centuries earlier. Those minor inconveniences don't seem to matter to him, though. Why should they? When we're in that space between, time and distance don't exist. We create these concepts when we're human so we can sort things out a bit easier. When we're in bodies we need all the help we can get, even from limiting illusions.

1

The phone is ringing. Insistent. Demanding. I don't really know why he has a phone in his office because he never uses it. Arlene, a perky little lady with short, blonde-gray hair and a great smile, always answers the phone from her desk in the reception area. I guess she's his secretary, although that word doesn't really fit their relationship, whatever it is. Perhaps they're business associates. Arlene sets up appointments for people to come and see him because he never talks to anyone on the phone. Ever. There isn't any kind of intercom system between the reception area and his office, so Arlene never even calls him on his phone to let him know someone is waiting to see him. She always comes into his office to deliver messages or to tell him he has a visitor. Not very efficient, but the arrangement seems to work just fine for them.

His office is very plain. No fancy décor. A few faded travel posters with slightly curled edges are pasted to the walls, and a large map of the solar system is taped to the wall between two of the posters. The slightly yellowed map looks like it's been there forever; edges are torn, and the print is faded and difficult to read. His desk – a large piece of carved oak – sits below the map, and a huge globe squats almost in the center of the room. An eclectic collection of folding chairs is scattered randomly throughout the office. The room actually looks like an old movie set rather than the functioning office of a travel agent.

There are six others waiting with me in the room. They aren't impatient though; they're just sitting or standing in various attitudes of anticipation. I take a seat near the door so I can indulge in my favorite game of trying to guess identities and destinations. Sometimes I recognize people, but other times I have no idea who anyone is, and I can't always figure out where people are going either. Often I can hear bits and pieces of conversation, and that sometimes helps me to discover destinations.

I listen to the two standing closest to me on my left. The woman, a striking, dark-haired beauty with lovely hands, is anxious about her journey. She wears a full length, pale yellow ruffled gown, and she holds a colorful fan in her right hand. Thick black hair, swept back from her face, is coiled and held in place by an elaborate comb. As I watch her I can almost hear guitar music. Spanish maybe? I lean a bit closer to see if I can confirm my guess and catch just a few of her words.

"I really feel like I want to go to England, Arturo. I promised Betsy I would be with her for a while, and I won't stay very long. I'd like to be with you, but I know you don't want to be there right now. I don't know what to do."

Arturo. Probably Spanish too. He wears knee-high boots and sports a thick mustache that compliments long, curly black hair. He offers reassurance and tells the woman that they can eventually see each other. "Just enjoy your stay in England, Consuela. After awhile you can join me in the United States. Somewhere in the western part of the country I think."

Seems like a simple plan to me. I wonder why she's so worried. She's actually wringing her hands and twisting the beautiful diamond rings that circle the ring finger on her left hand. Are they married? If so, why go separate ways? Now I'm confused.

I'm about to interrupt their conversation with a few nosy questions, but my attention is diverted by a thin, bald-headed man seated to my right. A long, straggly gray mustache that looks like an untrimmed goatee droops down to his breast bone. A tan robe, held in place by a brown silk sash, drapes his body. He doesn't say anything, but I can feel his energy. His face is familiar, but I can't quite remember his name, although I'm sure we've met before. I begin to stare rather obviously, and the more I look, the more I feel certain that we do know each other. Finally he smiles and then I know. Of course. Ho Yung. I want to ask where he's going, but that would be cheating. My little game has certain rules, and asking direct questions isn't allowed. I have to guess, otherwise it isn't fair. I'll have to wait on that one, so I return his smile and go back to my watching and eavesdropping.

I always find it interesting that even though many of us at Home know each other – and have even shared lives together– when we come to visit our travel agent it's as if those connections are suspended while we're in the room. I don't quite get what's going on about that; must remember to ask Clarence about it sometime. Very curious.

Directly across the room two others are standing near the desk. I can't hear them at all, but their body language tells me that they're having some sort of disagreement. A heavyset man wearing a loose fitting gray jacket, pin-striped pants, black vest, and white shirt with very starched collar is leaning on a cane. He's impatient with a woman who looks like she's just stepped out of the chorus line at the Moulin Rouge. The lady's bright red hair sticks out in every direction, and her dress is a dance hall costume that has definitely seen better days. Her gestures are disconnected and random, while her companion stands so stiff and reserved he hardly moves at all. A strange pair. It seems clear that they've come from different places, and I can't imagine how they know each other, much less be interested in traveling together.

A small woman with blonde wavy hair is seated alone near the wall on the left. Her only jewelry is a long pearl necklace, which falls gracefully over a pink, satin dress. She sits calmly, just waiting for the meeting to come to order. Well, it actually isn't really a meeting, but it feels like that at the moment. She's also a familiar face, and I know that she recognizes me too because when I catch her eye she waves and grins mischievously. I remember that look, and as I return her smile I have a fleeting image of the two of us walking together in some familiar place. Friends.

My daydreaming is interrupted when a particularly large plume of smoke erupts behind the desk, and he stands up. All conversation stops. It's always this way. He has a way of commanding attention without ever really saying very much, if anything. All eyes focus on him. He looks rather like an amalgamation of Santa Claus, Alfred Hitchcock and Orson Welles. Bushy mutton chops reach up to touch his sandy brown hair, which always looks a bit windblown. He wears the same tan jacket and brown tweed pants that he always wears, and the ever present gold watch makes a slight bulge in his vest pocket. His eyes dance as they take in the room, and he shows us a slight smile that promises a laugh is soon to be heard. He has a great laugh, and I can hardly wait to hear it again.

Cigar in hand, he walks around to the front of the desk and looks around the room. We all know he's waiting for us to speak, so we look at each other to see who will be first to talk. These aren't ever private conversations, and we all know that, so it isn't a matter of not wanting anyone else to hear what we have to say. It's more a question of who will begin. We're all here for the same reason, more or less, and he knows that. He just confirms reservations and helps us organize our itineraries.

He senses that we're reluctant to speak, so he begins to move around the room, greeting each of us. He always uses very formal English, flavored with a rich Scottish accent. I love listening to him speak and often wish that he would talk about himself and his travels, but he always tells me information about him isn't important. Playing the perfect host, he greets everyone, establishing contact, reassuring us that he's happy to see us. We need that, I think, because even though those who come to see him always have these talks with him, each time we need to know that we're welcome. Such creatures of habit we are, needing the security of tradition and ritual so we're able to venture into different territory without too much fear and anxiety.

CLARENCE

*There are many places to be, and the choices
are your own.*

As he makes his way over to me I stand up and get ready to greet him. The physical contact is important too. Not to him but to us. To me. Probably some sort of energy transference is necessary. At any rate, when he finally stands in front of me I reach out and shake his hand as he speaks to me. Actually, I really want to hug him, but he's pretty formal most of the time, so I settle for a handshake.

"Well, Ardeth, I see that you are on your way again."

"Good evening, Clarence. Good to see you again. Yes, I think I'm ready, but I just want to talk with you before I leave."

He smiles, nods, releases my hand, and then starts to move on to the next person. I'm reluctant to let go, and he senses this as he gives my hand a gentle pat before he moves away. Such a kind man. Always very intuitive.

After he's acknowledged everyone, Clarence goes back to his desk and disappears behind it just long enough to move his chair out in front of the desk so he can sit with us. He isn't a great one for barriers, even though he'd been invisible behind the stacks of folders on his desk when I first entered the room. That little tactic is just something he does while he waits for us to get settled.

His chair is really most distinctive. The arms, legs and high back of the chair are beautifully carved, and the soft padding of the seat and back are covered in a velvety blue-gray material. It looks like a very comfortable chair, but he's the only one who ever sits in it, so I really wouldn't know. The chair is the only fancy piece of furniture in the room. Even the large, sturdy desk is quite plain.

He sits down, plants both feet firmly in front of him, puts his cigar in his mouth, folds his hands over his ample waist, and waits.

We all draw our chairs closer to him so we're arranged in a circle. After much shuffling and re-arranging, everyone is quiet again. For a moment.

"I'm not sure…really, I'm not. Maybe I'd better stay for a while. I can't decide where to go. I only know that I want to be with Arturo."

"I'd like to build some houses."

"I need to be with other people. My time of quiet must be over so I can apply my lessons."

"I certainly don't want to go through that same awful thing again!"

"There are too many people there. I knew that would happen. I tried to tell them."

"I'm really excited about my trip. I can hardly wait."

"I want to write a book."

We're all talking at the same time. Once the initial silence is broken, fragmented thoughts and feelings bounce around the room. Clarence lets us ramble on for a few moments without interrupting, knowing we'll eventually realize that there isn't any conversation happening. We do, and the comments gradually fade as we finally notice that everybody is talking, but nobody is listening. Except Clarence. He always listens very carefully.

"All right, lads and lassies. You have come to tell me about your journeys, and that is fine. I can be of help to you, but there are many places to be, and the choices are your own. To be sure, your visits can be scheduled any way you like, but we must first have a time of reflection. Think these thoughts: Where are you now? Where have you been? Have you been learning your lessons? Where are you going?"

He leans back, takes a contented puff of his cigar and again waits. A most patient man.

"Well, I'm feeling nervous about this whole thing, so I'd like to talk first if that's agreeable to everyone."

CONSUELA

Listen to yourself and understand what you have learned from your experiences.

All eyes turn to the woman on my left. Her partner, Arturo, had called her Consuela when I was listening to them earlier. I look again at those lovely hands and wonder if she ever does any gardening. An absurd and irrelevant thought, but it just pops into my head. She doesn't look real, and yet there's an earthy quality about her that seems to hover just around the edges of her beautifully made up face and exquisitely styled hair. Curious.

"...and so, I really don't know what to do."

"Consuela, I would ask you this. What is it you want to do?"

"It's not that simple, Clarence. I know where I've been. I remember all too clearly my last visit—large outdoor ovens that were like great bee hives, the smell of baking bread, a long journey with the dark-skinned ones, the cave, our son's arrival, Arturo's leaving—I remember it all, and I just don't know."

"But lass, what are you remembering? If your thoughts are resting only with people and events, you will never come close to what you have learned from your last visit. Look within, Consuela. Listen to yourself and understand what you have learned from your experiences."

"But I can't seem to understand. The lessons have been clearer before, and now I feel too unsure of myself to know what to do next. I feel like I'll miss something terribly important if I delay any longer; yet, I don't feel confident of where I'm going or why I'm going there, other than the promise to be with Betsy, who will be my mother during this visit."

"Consuela, let me ask you this. Can you see your own back?"

"My back? Do you mean can I physically see it? No."

"Yet, you must know it is there, correct? You can feel it, even though you must use a mirror to see it. Trust your feelings, lass."

"I don't know. I suppose I do seem to have a hard time trusting myself, don't I? I'll try to do better. I just hope there won't be any frogs near me this time. That experience was so upsetting I can hardly say the word."

"Frogs? Oh, come now, lass. You need not keep that with you. Why carry old baggage that is no longer necessary? There is no need to be doing that again."

I'm not sure I'm hearing her correctly, but Clarence repeated the word, so I know that's what she must have said. Frogs. I can't imagine where all of this is going. What do frogs have to do with anything?

"...but I can still hear the sound of their muffled croaking, vibrating every lily pad that clustered around me as I sank. It was horrible!"

At this point, Clarence gets up and walks over to her. He takes both of her hands in his and gently pulls her to her feet. Without releasing her hands, he begins to talk to her in a quiet but authoritative voice.

"Consuela, listen to me. What is done is done. To continue to carry old griefs with you only slows your progress. Understand that you chose to leave under the orchestration of the frog voices, and you need not continue those memories. They hold no meaning for you any longer. Think about what you have learned. Think about the lessons you have chosen for yourself that are yet to be completed. Apply those memories to a useful end."

Clarence lets go of her hands, walks back to his chair, and sits down. We all watch Consuela to see what she will do. There doesn't seem to be enough air in the room at this moment.

Consuela stands for just a bit longer, and then she sits down too. And she smiles.

"Thank you, Clarence. I hadn't realized how much of that I still carry with me. It was so awful I have a hard time forgetting, but you're right. I must let go of that experience."

"Consuela, just make your decision and get on with it, please. If you're not sure you want to go, stay here. You don't have to go anywhere."

Arturo speaks gently but firmly. He doesn't seem to have any problems knowing what he's doing.

"Oh no, I'm going wherever you go...eventually. I'll spend time with the English family, and then I can join you later. But I absolutely refuse to budge until you tell me where we can meet."

Arturo gives her a kind of lop-sided grin. "Well, we could always be twins. That way you'll always know where I am."

"Oh, no, my darling. That's not what I had in mind at all. I want to be your wife again."

Arturo takes her hand. "All right. Why not meet near the old home ground? Surely you'll remember that when the time comes."

"Fine. Just as long as I know. Clarence, you will be here when we return, won't you?"

"Perhaps, lassie, but I may be visiting other places too, and then you may have another travel agent."

"No, I don't want another agent. I want you."

As Consuela speaks, my imagination quickly conjures up an image of a petulant child who's about to stamp her feet, but to her credit Consuela doesn't have a tantrum. She hears her own words and amends her comments.

"Well, I suppose I could adjust. When can I leave? I need to get on with this."

Clarence reaches behind his chair and selects a folder from the pile on top of his desk. It's amazing that he can find anything in that mass of papers and books, but he seems to have a system of organization that works for him. He opens the folder and studies the contents for a moment.

"You may leave whenever you like, of course. You are the best judge of that. The information you have provided tells me that you will be able to go directly, without a great deal of difficulty. We've talked of this before. Just remember that the journey can be a tedious one, so you must be prepared for that."

Tedious! What an understatement. Getting there is the one part of visiting that I don't like. All of that banging around while traveling down the long Chute always gives me a headache. Tedious, indeed. More like difficult, painful, and more adjectives than I'm able to conjure up at the moment.

Consuela glances over at Arturo as she reluctantly stands up. This lady is definitely dragging her feet.

"Wait, lass. You might benefit from listening to the others. It is not necessary to leave right this moment. Time is not important now. You can be putting it to good use later. Rest and stay for a bit." Clarence knows she's stalling and wants to give her an opportunity to collect her thoughts. Very considerate.

Consuela sits down as Clarence closes the folder, puts it back on the desk, and then turns to look at the rest of us. He gives us that impish grin of his and waits for someone else to speak.

ARTURO

…and so you have created your own reality, as we all do.

"As Consuela said, I don't care about going to England. I'd like to first visit the place called Minnesota, where friends are living. Then, I think that I can best continue my building near the old homestead. There are many opportunities there for me to learn more and to build again. I've been away from building for such a long time, since the first visit, really. The waterways and underground channels on Crete were an exciting challenge, and I'd like to build again. Maybe not waterways, but some kind of construction."

Clarence listens intently, nodding occasionally. I can see a question coming.

"Arturo, let me ask, if I may. Have you come to understand why building is so important to you?"

"I'm not sure, but it's probably some kind of outward reassurance that I'm accomplishing something. I'm a very ordinary being, really, and I think I must need physical evidence of a completed task to let me know that growth is taking place. Maybe I'm just kidding myself, but I don't know if anything is really happening unless I can see it. If I build something I know it must be real because I can see it in front of me. Does that make any sense?"

"Of course, my friend. Of course it does. You have made it happen, and so you have created your own reality, as we all do. And then, too, you are dealing with a symbol you understand. Your ability to build on the outside comes from within, laddie. Perhaps there will even come a day when the need to see the fruits of your labor will no longer be necessary. You will just know what you have accomplished without any tangible evidence."

"Maybe so, but for now the need to build is there. I want my journey to take me to places where I can do that. Soon, I think."

There doesn't seem to be any need for Clarence to check Arturo's file. He simply nods and turns to the rest of us.

We've all been listening to the conversations, and the need to speak doesn't seem very urgent to anyone. Listening can be a passive art, and I suppose we're just relaxing into the role of listeners quite easily. There might also be a degree of avoidance there. At least for me.

Clarence finally breaks the silence. "Ho Yung, are you ready?"

HO YUNG

The understanding you have now may escape you for a time,
but your ability to look within will never leave,
and the confusion will pass.

I turn to the familiar face on my right. Wherever he's been, there was a tranquility there that's stayed with him. A peaceful man. As I look at him, waiting for him to respond to Clarence's question, I catch a glimpse of flames. Odd. The image passes quickly, and a serene landscape replaces it. I see sheep quietly grazing on green hills. What intriguing contradictory images. I wish I could remember him. After a bit, Ho Yung speaks.

23

"Yes, I'm ready. I know that my life of solitude is complete for now, and the world of art and plants must be my home for a time. In the journey ahead I feel there will be many opportunities for application of other lessons learned, and also for growth in many areas. There are so many paths to choose, and communication with others involving you, Clarence, seems to be an important road for me to follow. There may be people who will not understand that path because of the times I have chosen, but I must accept that. I may very well forget the understanding that I have too. It is so easy to get caught up in the moment, the movement, the activities. I may need help from you if I choose to walk the path of communications. May I call on you if I need assistance?"

Well, that's a long speech. Ho Yung speaks precisely and clearly, and it's obvious that he thinks out his words before he says them. I have questions about many of his statements, just as I have with what Consuela and Arturo have said, but I don't think that this is the right time to voice them. There are too many bits and pieces of information flying around right now. Maybe later.

Clarence nods and indulges in a slight laugh. I notice that he doesn't call Ho Yung "lad" or "laddie." "Of course. If, as you say, you become too caught up in the moment, I may have to call upon you. You could very well resist that too. The understanding you have now may escape you for a time, but your ability to look within will never leave, and the confusion will pass. Perhaps at those times you will hear me. Also, it would be good if you tried to remember to be at peace with the vehicle you have chosen for your visit. I say this only because on your last trip you made such a determined effort to overcome the apparent limitations of being in a body."

Ho Yung smiles. He's so calm and relaxed it's hard to think of him ever being so caught up in a situation that he might resist, or to imagine that he might need assistance. He seems so self-assured. I notice too that there's no discussion at all about his departure. He seems to know about that too. The more I think about him, the more I wish I could remember how we know each other, but all I get are elusive images that don't make sense. Fire and sheep aren't exactly compatible. Perhaps I can talk with him later.

THOMAS

To judge others according to your values only places you in
shoes that do not fit because they do not belong to you.

My thoughts are interrupted by a rather loud "harrumph."
I'm not exactly sure that "harrumph" is a word that accurately
describes the sound made when clearing the throat, but that's
what it sounds like. "Harrumph."

The heavyset man with the cane is definitely getting ready
to speak. He fusses nervously with his collar and begins to
address Clarence. As he starts to talk, I groan inwardly because
I've heard that tone of voice before. Pedantic. Authoritative.
Annoying.

"Now, Clarence, I think it's time to get on with matters that involve me. It's not that I'm disinterested in the rest of you people, but my immediate area of concern is my impending journey, which, frankly, I'm not looking forward to at all. The whole idea of joining the teeming masses again is rather abhorrent, especially since they didn't listen to me during my last visit. Why would I have reason to believe it will be any different this time?"

My, my, he really does stuff his shirt rather nicely. I can't help but smile, and yet there's that faint twinge of something familiar in his voice that makes me vaguely uncomfortable. A disturbing echo comes from inside of me. I dismiss the uneasy feeling and turn to see how Clarence will respond to him.

"Thomas, I would ask you this. Did you have anything instructive to offer people?"

"Well, I should think so. After all, my solution was really quite logical. Why wouldn't the voice of common sense be worth hearing? It seems only reasonable that someone who has the answer to a difficult question would be heard."

"Perhaps, but you may have been trying to solve someone else's problem with your solution. You can speak only for yourself. To judge others according to your values only places you in shoes that do not fit because they do not belong to you."

Uh-oh. Could be trouble.

Thomas stands up, and it seems for a moment that he might leave the room. He's very clearly not happy with the way this conversation is going. We all watch him, expecting almost anything except what happens next.

Just as quickly as he'd gotten to his feet, Thomas sits down and begins to laugh. I stare in amazement as his laughter fills the room. Clarence begins to chuckle, and soon we're all laughing. I doubt that we understand why we've joined the hilarity, but we certainly have. It seems like the right thing to do, and it feels good to laugh.

Finally Thomas speaks again, but this time I don't hear that familiar, self-important tone of voice. He delivers his words calmly, with a degree of wonder.

"I amaze myself sometimes. I really do. I know what you're thinking, Clarence. I don't have to go if I don't want to leave; I know that. But I also began to realize as I listened to myself speak that I still have a great deal to learn. I think I need to continue my time of reflection before I go for another visit. Some lessons apparently take longer than others to learn."

"Aye, Thomas, that is true. Do not try to move beyond where you are at the moment until you are ready. We all learn at our own pace. Be patient."

"I will, Clarence. But I do have one more question. Why are there so many more people each time I visit? I don't understand where they all come from. Why are there always more?"

"Well, my friend, if you have an area large enough to accommodate many people, they will naturally be there. There is no shortage of spirits wishing to visit."

"But the size of the area we're talking about hasn't changed. It's always been like it is. Where were they before?"

"Other places, of course. You do not really think that there is just one place to be, do you?"

"Well, I hadn't thought about there being other places before, so I suppose I did think there was only one place to be. Tell me then, Clarence, if there are other places, could we...could I go to another place sometime for a visit?"

"Certainly, Thomas." A pause and then a slight smile. "Are you not visiting another place right now?"

LOUISE

The only signposts on the road are those you place there.

Thomas's companion is staring at him. Her mouth is open, and she's wide-eyed and incredulous. Frowzy red hair that looks as though it hasn't been attended to in some time frames a face that shows the ravages of dissipation. Her worn out body has clearly seen much better days. Wherever she's been, it's obviously been an ordeal for her, and if she's been involved in some sort of conflict, I can't tell who won by looking at her. It's only apparent that she seems to have fought well.

"Louise, why are you surprised at your friend's comments?"

Clarence sits back and re-lights his cigar because it keeps going out on him.

"Why wouldn't I be surprised? I've never heard him laugh before. I mean, never. I was beginning to think he had no sense of humor, just like all of the other serious ones in Montmartre. Always glaring, but never too serious for a quick pinch under the table. Oh no, that's different. Mean, they are. Just plain mean. At least some of them. No joy in their lives. Desperate. All of them. They disgust me. And yet, I pity them. They have no music in their souls. None."

The woman called Louise speaks in quick, jerky half sentences. Words come pouring out in random fits and starts. Fascinating. She pities them, whoever "them" might be. There's fire in her eyes when she speaks, and I begin to realize that she isn't worn out at all. Her appearance is merely a façade; her costume is just window dressing. Interesting thought. I wonder what I look like to her, but I know if I ask her she'll most certainly tell me, and I'm not sure I'm ready for the answer. At least not before I hear more of what she has to say. And she does have more to say.

"Balance, that's it. And joy. Yes, definitely joy. Unfortunately, on my last visit I overindulged – I emptied my glass too quickly – and everyone else's. The music played too fast. Much too fast. I know that now, and I'm anxious to continue the dance, but at a more moderate pace. Perhaps ballet. What do you think, Clarence?"

Louise punctuates her question by standing up, performing a rather awkward but determined pirouette, and landing somewhat ungracefully back in her chair.

Clarence suppresses a smile. "Louise, more important than what I think is what you feel. If you wish to do the dance, then you will. The only sign posts on the road are those that you place there. There are many ways to dance. If you feel you have learned what you need to know from your last visit, then you must decide what to do next. What I think is not important."

"Not important?" She's indignant. "Now see here, my friend. All of those nasty cigars you smoke have gone to your head and clouded your vision. What you think is very important. I know you can't make decisions for me, but I value your opinion. Otherwise I wouldn't be here. So, tell me. What do you think?"

"All right, lass. All right. When you say 'balance,' what do you mean?"

Again, all eyes turn to Louise. I'm especially interested in her answer for reasons of my own. She pauses, in what I assume to be a moment of reflection, but considering her appearance she seems to be almost posing as a caricature of herself.

"Balance is…balance. What more can I say? It's knowing that for every scowl there's a smile to counteract it. For every action there's a reaction. It's harmony. That's it. Harmony. Notes that blend. Colors that flow. Sounds that mix to make music. Just the right amount of everything."

"Aye, lassie, that is very good. But how do you know when you have, as you say, the *right amount*?"

"How do you know? You listen, that's how. You feel it. You know, that's all. It's just there. And, you can tell when it's not the right amount. My last visit was a procession of clashing cymbals. It's knowing how to make the notes blend that's the trick. That's the hard part. You have to listen to do it right. I didn't listen enough. I was too busy reacting to understand that I could act on my own choices. I forgot."

I'm stunned. Underneath that dance hall girl is a poet. Beautiful music dances in her soul. I like her.

It's apparent that Clarence does too, because he smiles broadly and reaches back for yet another folder that's right at his fingertips. "Louise, the music you desire can be found in many places. Do you wish a direct flight, or will you be taking a leisurely tour before you arrive at your destination?"

"Oh, I think maybe a tour. I'm not in any particular hurry. I have some recuperating to do before I go charging off again. Some time in the sun would be nice, and there are a few other people I'd like to visit on the way. Just book me on the milk run, and I'll be perfectly content."

"Fine. We will arrange things as you wish."

WEE BET

I guess it's a little bit like trying to take someone else's bath for him. It's just not possible.

The only person in the room who hasn't spoken yet, other than me, is the blonde-haired woman seated near the wall to my left. She looks over at me with a question in her mischievous eyes. I give her a *be my guest* signal, and she responds with a smile and a wink. Once again I have that fleeting image of the two of us walking together somewhere near water. She's a dark skinned man, and I'm wearing robes. I feel as though I've known her for a very long time.

"Hi, Clarence. It's wonderful to see you. I've been so eager to talk with you because I feel like I have so much to do. The world is such an exciting place, and there are all kinds of people I'd like to see. I really want to help people."

Clarence returns her impish grin with one of his own. "Hi to you, Wee Bet."

I've never heard Clarence say "hi" to anyone before. Delightful. The word sounds very strange coming from him, but he looks as though he's enjoying himself. He's such an adaptable fellow he can probably speak Portuguese too.

"And how is it that you wish to be of help, lass?"

"Oh, I can think of all kinds of ways, but mostly I think with my healing abilities. I like to see people whole. Life is too wonderful not to enjoy it, and being sick is such a waste of time and energy. What do you think, Clarence? How do you think I can be of the most help?"

"Wee Bet, to answer your question, allow me to ask you to imagine that you have been asked to accompany a friend to a particular place. You do not have any special desire to go to this place, but you walk with your friend because he has asked you to join him."

Clarence waits a moment, looking for a nod of understanding from Wee Bet. As I watch her, I think about her name. Wee Bet is a perfect name for her. She's diminutive in size, and if Elizabeth is her given name, it's too long. Bet, or even Wee Bet, is much better.

She nods. "That's easy, because I've done just that many times."

"Good. Let us say that at a certain point in your walk, you come to a crossroads. Your friend is not sure which road to take; he has become very tired, and for some reason that is not clear to you, he is apprehensive. He knows that one of the two roads will lead to his destination, but he can not decide which road to take. And, more importantly, he does not feel up to continuing the journey. He asks you to decide for him which road to take, and then to continue without him. How do you respond?"

I can see that Wee Bet is caught up in the story, as we all are, and she answers immediately. "But Clarence, if I leave him there at the crossroads while I continue to walk, what will he do? I can't just leave him there if he isn't feeling well."

Clarence nods. "He reassures you that he will be fine. He says he will simply wait for you to return."

"Well, if I were sure that he would be comfortable just waiting for me, I would do as he asks. If he's too tired to continue, I've got to try to help by going on without him."

"Just so." Clarence continues. "You make the decision for him and take the road that leads to the west. You have made a practical choice, and you find yourself in the place your friend described earlier. Once there, what do you do?"

"I would probably feel happy that I had made the right choice, and then I would...I would...." She stops right there, a puzzled look on her face. "I don't know what I would do. I don't know why he wanted to go to that place. I didn't ask. How silly of me!"

"Why do you suppose you did not think to ask what his mission was before you left him, Wee Bet?"

"I don't know, Clarence. I suppose I was just caught up in completing the journey for him. I was in a hurry because I knew he was waiting. As I walked I could see him sitting there. He looked tired and perhaps a bit afraid, so I was anxious to do what he wanted me to do."

"But what have you gained? You have arrived at the place your friend said he wanted to be, but because he is not with you, you do not know why you are there. He needed to either continue by himself or walk with you at his side. You cannot accomplish his mission for him because you do not know what it is. You could only have been of help if he had come with you on the walk."

Wee Bet smiles in understanding. "Well, I'll be.... Of course! I guess it's a little bit like trying to take someone else's bath for him. It's just not possible. That's a wonderful story, Clarence. Thanks."

"You are most welcome, lass. And will you be leaving soon?"

Wee Bet thinks for a moment, and then she gets up and begins to walk around the room. She pauses in front of Arturo and holds out her hand to him. He takes it, but I can tell he isn't quite sure what she's doing. She holds his hand and gives it a squeeze. He responds with a smile, and I think he's about to ask her a question, but she moves away before he can speak. When she returns to her chair, she answers Clarence's question.

"I thought so before we started to talk, but I think I'll stay here for a while. Before Arturo begins to build he might want to visit places I've been, and I may be able to help."

Then, she turns to me and answers the question I have in my head, but haven't voiced out loud. "Oh, sure, Ardeth. We'll walk together again if you like."

Now they're all looking at me. I return her smile and nod because I really can't think of a response. I look over at Clarence and he's re-lighting his cigar again. People who smoke cigars seem to spend a great deal of time lighting them, which makes me wonder why they don't stay lit. Finally, the cigar tip begins to glow, and he looks at me and nods.

My turn. My role of observer has temporarily come to a halt. Everyone is waiting to hear what I have to say.

ARDETH

You may very well have good words to say,
but you must allow those who hear you to choose
whether or not you speak to them.

"Well, Clarence, I'm almost reluctant to speak. I think I have more questions now than when I entered the room. I hardly know where to begin." Typical. I always have more questions than answers.

"Aye, Ardeth. Please go on."

By now he's used to my questions. I always find it interesting that I seem to end up answering my own questions by the time we're through talking. That's the thing about Clarence; he has such a marvelous facility for asking questions that provide a means for me to answer my own questions. I hesitate just long enough for him to speak again.

"Well, then, lassie, I will ask my question first. Why have you come?"

That's simple. I can answer that one. "To say hi (I can't resist) and to tell you that I'll be on my way soon. Also, to see if it's all right to use your name in the book I'd like to write."

"What kind of a book is it that you wish to write, Ardeth?"

"I want to share what I've learned, Clarence. When I observe people, including myself on the rare occasion that I can be objective about me, I've come up with some thoughts that might be of help to others. Since you've been so instrumental in my learning process, I'd like to be able to use your name when I talk about what you've taught me."

I get a big smile. It isn't quite a patronizing smile, because Clarence is never patronizing, but almost. Fatherly, perhaps. I have a feeling that my foot has found its way into my mouth again. Oh well, it won't be the first time.

"Lassie, I would ask you the same question I asked Thomas. What makes you think you have anything to say that others will find helpful or be of any interest?"

I know that one is coming, and I'm prepared for it.

"Well, Clarence, I think what you have to say is always helpful and interesting. Why wouldn't others feel the same way?"

I think I've handled that one nicely, which shows how much I know, and so I'm really taken aback when he laughs. It isn't a chuckle, either. He really laughs.

"Lassie, lassie, come now. Listen to yourself. Why would your book, even if it is about me, be of interest to anyone else? You and Thomas over there have something in common here. You presume to know what is best for others. That cannot be.

As Wee Bet said, everyone must take his own bath."

He has me going. "Oh, Clarence, c'mon. That's not what I'm saying at all. I don't want to tell others how to live. I know better than that. That trip to the Canary Islands taught me at least that much. After the natives set me adrift on that unholy raft I had plenty of time to think about what I had tried to do. I didn't see it at the time, but the experience on the raft gave me an opportunity to evaluate the whole visit, and I learned that I had no right to interfere. I had no answers for others. I know that now."

"Then, why write the book, Ardeth?"

"Why? I've just told you why. To teach. To tell a story. To share what I've learned. Perhaps to amuse people. Whatever."

"But what makes you think you have anything to teach?"

This conversation is going in circles. I feel like I'm being perfectly clear, and yet he doesn't seem to understand me. Or does he? I give it another try.

"Look, Clarence, I just want to write a book about where we are now. People can read the book if they choose to do so and interpret it any way they like. The book may never get published, but if it does perhaps no one will buy it, and therefore no one will read it. I won't be forcing anything on anyone."

I guess my voice raises a notch on that last comment because when I finish everyone is really staring at me. I'm not having a good time at all. I'd walked into the room thinking that I'd just pay a short call, ask about using his name in the book, and then be on my way. Instead, here I am, knee deep in a very circular conversation. Definitely not fun. And, it isn't over yet.

"Why write a book that no one will read?" Clarence is really persistent.

I feel like I'm wading through molasses. Enough of this.

"Okay, Clarence, what is it you're trying to say? I know there must be a point to this conversation, otherwise we wouldn't be having it, but I'm lost. I've come to ask a simple question. Why are you making things so complicated?"

"Ardeth, I'm trying to say that you can speak only for yourself and not for others. I want to be sure you know that. You may very well have good words to say, but you must allow those who hear you to choose whether or not you speak to them. You must make it possible for those who read your book to read it in any way that is comfortable for them. I want you to hear yourself saying the words you have said."

That makes sense. He always does. "Oh...well, I'm hearing myself, and I do feel I know what I want to do."

There's a rather awkward pause. It feels as if the session is over, yet I think we're all reluctant to leave. I know I want to stay a bit longer, and I sense the others feel the same. There seems to be so much more to say. I rather like these people, and I want to talk more with them.

Clarence looks as though he's ready to retreat behind his desk, and yet I don't feel like my conversation with him is complete either. He still hasn't answered my question about using his name in the book.

I don't have time to pursue this line of thought because right then the door opens, and a woman catapults into the room. I use this word deliberately, because to say that she walks into the room would be misleading. She doesn't simply enter the room. The door flies open, and she's here. Breathless. Bits of paper are clutched in her right hand; her eyes are wide open, and she has what might be a perpetual look of surprise on her face. Light brown hair swirls around her head in a swarm of curls. She's a mass of energy looking for a place to be.

DOROTHY

I feel like I've been caught sideways in a tornado.

"I'm late I know I am I tried to get here on time really I did but I just couldn't seem to get organized I was halfway here and I remembered that I had notes I wanted to bring so I went back to get them then just outside I saw the most fantastic *Antennaria parvifolia* actually its common name is Nuttall's Pussytoes and I just had to stop and study it and well here I am...am I too late?"

"Come in, Dorothy. It is very nice to see you again. No, you are not too late. Please be comfortable." Clarence, the gentleman. I think he could graciously receive a rhinoceros that had stumbled into a formal dinner party. Greeting this whirlwind of energy and words is easy for him because he never judges or editorializes about anything. He just smiles.

I know who she is too. I've read everything her brother William has written, and I'm familiar with some of her poetry as well. I hadn't expected to see her here, but I'm pleased to have the opportunity to meet her. I indicate a chair near me, and she drops into it. She seems scattered and excited.

"I hope I'm not interrupting anyone."

Dorothy looks around the room. Quick glances take everyone in. No one really has a chance to respond before words come flying out of her mouth again. "Good. Clarence I can't wait to tell you I'm going first to Iowa and then perhaps to a more temperate climate I'm going to work with flowers growing them I've always wanted to do that and it's time I have the plans for my garden right here look aren't they wonderful don't you think this will make a marvelous garden I'll be able to grow miniature gladiolus the unusual varieties marigold wonderful color all kinds of tulips and daffodils of course everything isn't it marvelous?"

During this breathless monologue Dorothy has moved from her chair to the desk where Clarence had been standing when she'd entered the room. As she talks, she ushers him to his chair and literally knocks the cigar out of his mouth with the papers she's waving in her hand. I don't think she's even aware of what she's done, but before he has a chance to react, she bends over, picks up the cigar, puts it back in his mouth, and never misses a beat in her enthusiastic ramblings. By the time Clarence is seated she's dumped her pieces of paper in his lap and is bending over his shoulder, talking the whole time.

I don't remember Dorothy being described as a talker, but then I haven't heard about her for some time. She's obviously been on a number of visits since her stay in Grasmere, and she certainly doesn't seem to be a shadow figure like she was there any longer.

While we're all still recovering from her enthusiastic announcements, Dorothy is on her way out the door.

"Dorothy, wait. Stay and talk with us. I am sure those who are here would like to hear more about your plans." Crumpled cigar in hand, Clarence is on his feet again.

"Oh thank you Clarence but I really can't stay now but if you'd all like to join me in the meadow I'd love to show you a most unique *Fritillaria lanceolata* that I found there earlier this morning it's just beautiful the intricacy is truly a work of art."

With that parting comment, Dorothy is gone. I feel as though I've been caught sideways in a tornado. I look around and notice that the others don't appear to be any more settled than I. Clarence looks at us and makes a suggestion.

"Well, friends, shall we walk? We can continue our conversation on the way. A wee bit of fresh air might be a nice change right now in the wake of our exuberant Dorothy, who is a bit like a burst of sunlight herself. We can join her in the meadow."

Clarence begins to move toward the door, and we all get up and prepare to follow him. He leaves first, followed by Wee Bet, Ho Yung and me, since we're closest to the door. Arturo, Consuela, Thomas and Louise aren't far behind.

THE LANE

FOLLOW THE LEADER

...it's difficult to just be in the moment.

After we leave Clarence's office, we walk through the reception area where Arlene is busy talking on the phone. She smiles and waves at us as we parade past her into the corridor. I'd like to invite her to join us, but I think the invitation might be a bit presumptuous since Clarence hasn't asked her to come along. It'd be fun to have her with us though. Her perkiness and Dorothy's enthusiasm would match each other nicely. Oh well, perhaps another time.

We continue down the corridor and out of the building, which itself is nondescript, really. There isn't any particular architectural flavor to it at all; it just seems to blend in rather organically with the landscape. Rather amorphous in design, neither interesting nor offensive. Just there. A part of the surroundings.

Once we leave the building, we begin walking down a lane shaded by large oak trees. The trees are so large that their tops form a natural canopy over the lane. Just beyond the oak trees, fields of mustard, gleaming bright yellow in the sun, flank the lane on both sides. Apple trees in full bloom sprout like large cotton candy sticks throughout the yellow fields. The fragrance of the apple blossoms is wonderful. It's a beautiful day. Just beautiful.

I don't know where we're going, but Clarence leads the way and we follow. I suppose we must look a bit like children playing follow the leader. Not a bad analogy, really, but as we continue our walk, my image of our little parade takes on more of a Canterbury Tales feeling as I hear bits and pieces of conversation drift through the morning air.

I think it's morning. It feels like we've been in Clarence's office most of the night, but he keeps rather unconventional office hours, and no one seems to mind that. As he'd said earlier, time isn't a concern here. It's hard to let go of the old habit of thinking in terms of time, though. Visits to places like Earth always seem to leave lingering impressions. The residual imprints are appropriate, I suppose, since we're here to reflect before we move on, but it's difficult to just be in the moment. Another lesson to be learned. Perhaps if I just think of this as a morning moment, I might be able to experience it more completely. Keep walking and savor the moment. Neat trick.

Wee Bet drops back a bit to talk with Arturo, and I can hear her asking him if he wants her to guide him for a while.

"Well, sure, little lady; that would be fine. I wasn't really certain that's what you had in mind back there when you took my hand, but please do. I've been a guide too, and I know that sometimes it's hard to get through to people who are experiencing a visit somewhere else. I tend to forget so much. What name will you use when you talk to me?"

"Anna, I think. I like that name and it feels right. We'll talk more later, but I just wanted to be sure it was okay with you. I get a little carried away sometimes, and I don't want to presume."

"No, not at all. I'll welcome your help, and perhaps I'll be able to return the favor someday."

Their conversation reminds me of my most recent experience as a guide. I've just completed it, as a matter of fact. I've been talking with a woman who works as a psychiatric nurse in an English hospital. A most difficult assignment, both hers and mine. She's quite receptive, really, but she's chosen a very unpleasant location for her lessons. Not because of the patients in the hospital, but because of the attitudes of those with whom she works. Diagnostic labels fly around as though they have very powerful wings. Any behavior out of the ordinary that is not understood is labeled as dangerous or abnormal. Celebrating diversity, or even tolerating it, isn't something humans do very well. There's too much ego, and even more fear involved in accepting differences.

Very odd, this tendency to categorize all of life so carefully. I understand the security in that system of pigeon-holing, but it really is limiting. But then, the limits are necessary for those who use them I suppose. At any rate, it's been a most difficult and interesting time for both of us. Someone else is working with her now because of my impending journey, and I hope they're doing well. Some lessons are so very hard.

My thoughts are interrupted by a kind of rustling sound. I look around and notice that someone, not part of our little group, is walking rapidly behind me. The rustling I hear comes from the black and white robes she's wearing. Penguin garb. She's in a hurry, whoever she is. As she's about to pass me, I think it only polite to greet her. After all, courtesy was expected when I was a part of the Order.

"Good morning, Sister. Lovely day, isn't it?"

"Good morning. Yes, it's a beautiful day. I...Elizabeth? Sister Elizabeth? Is that you? Is it really you?"

Mother Superior herself. How does she recognize me? I don't look like a nun any more. Or do I? Maybe what's seen depends on who's doing the looking.

"Yes, it's me. How good to see you again." The lie about it being good to see her again comes easily. Shame on me.

"You've been well, I hope, Sister? Staying out of trouble these days?"

Ouch. She hasn't forgotten. If the term renegade was ever applicable to a bride of Christ, that would have been the word used to describe me as a nun. I had a very difficult time of it. Practicing medicine without a priest in attendance was considered a sin, and I didn't always find it convenient to call for a priest when someone needed help. The pox was ravaging the country, and there wasn't always time. And, of course, most unfairly, I wanted it both ways. I wanted to wear the cloth, yet be allowed to practice my own brand of medicine and theology, even if the oath I had taken was in opposition to my values and practice. It never occurred to me that I should leave the Order rather than violate the vows I had taken. Well, I paid the piper on that one. Served me right.

I finally respond to her question. "Well, I'm trying. In retrospect, I'm grateful for your help. I know I didn't understand at the time, but I suppose that's always the way. You were very kind and I appreciate that. Where are you going?"

"I'm on my way to see my teacher. I'll be off soon to visit North Carolina, and I wanted to check my travel plans. Perhaps we'll have an opportunity to work together sometime in a more compatible frame of reference."

I wonder who her teacher is, but she seems to be in a hurry, so I just wish her well and she continues on her way. Interesting that we should meet again. Perhaps in another situation we might get along very well, and we could work together. Who knows? Dealing with a hard-headed, recalcitrant nun couldn't have been easy for her. She really didn't know what to do with me except continue to send me off to various convents, hoping I'd eventually shape up. I certainly hadn't been understanding of her position at the time and thought of her as inflexible and domineering, but perhaps in another setting with different lessons to learn we might do very well.

It feels like we've walked for quite awhile already. Here I am, doing it again, keeping track of time. Why can't I just enjoy the walk and not think about how long we've been walking? I'm muttering to myself as I catch up to Clarence and ask how far it is to the meadow.

"As far as you would like it to be, lassie." He continues to walk, hands in his pants' pockets. His cigar sticks out of his mouth like a piece of rolled bark. He has a new cigar because Dorothy's exuberance demolished his other one.

"As far as I want it to be? What does that mean?"

A Field of Water

Whatever I perceive, exists.

Clarence stops and points to the field on the right side of the lane. "Tell me what you see, Ardeth."

I look in the direction he's pointing and describe what I see beyond the grove of trees that shade the lane. "I see a golden carpet of yellow mustard. There are also some apple trees in the field." I guess we haven't walked very far after all because it looks like the same field I saw when we began our walk.

Clarence looks at me for a moment and then at the field. "Aye. Ardeth, what if I told you that I view the sea there? The sea is calm, and waves are gently greeting the shoreline. There are no trees. I do not see any mustard in the field. I see only water."

I stare at him to see if he's joking because sometimes it's hard to catch his sense of humor. I'm still smarting a bit from our conversation about the book, so I want to be sure he isn't teasing me. But he seems perfectly serious. I look again and see a field of mustard and apple trees. No water. "I would say that's not possible. There isn't any water there. You can't be seeing water. Can you?" Now I'm not sure.

"Of course I can, lassie. I can see anything I wish. Whatever I perceive, exists. It is very simple, really."

"But...." I don't know what to say. I know he's trying to tell me something important, but I can't grasp it. I don't see any water, but somehow I know if he says it's there, it is. I believe him, but I don't understand the meaning of his words.

"You believe me, do you not? It does not matter if we do not see the same scene. I can enjoy my ocean, and you, your field. We each create our own reality. And so, in answer to your original question, I can tell you that the meadow is as close or far away as you want it to be. Do you understand?"

"I think I understand about how we can see different things. A matter of perception, I suppose. I've just had an encounter with someone who sees me as a nun, but that's not how I see myself. In retrospect, and considering what you've just said about seeing water, I do understand what you're saying about that kind of perception. But I don't get how distance can be flexible. The meadow is a certain distance from where we are right now. It can't be as close or far away as I want it to be. It is where it is. And we are where we are." Am I about to wade in molasses again? Mentally, I begin to put on my hip boots.

"Ardeth, let me ask you this question. Have you ever walked while thinking, not of your destination, but of other matters?"

"Of course, Clarence. I do that all the time. My mind wanders, and I don't pay attention to where I'm going."

"Aye, just so. And then, when you reach your destination do you remember how you got there, and how long it took you to walk to that place?"

I see where he's going with this, or at least I think I do. "No, sometimes I'm surprised to find myself where I am, and I don't really remember how I got there, or how long it took me to walk whatever distance it was. But my errant thoughts don't influence the distance. Or, do they? Is that what you're saying? Distance is relative, depending on my frame of mind?"

"Aye, lassie. That is exactly what I am saying. If you are anxious about your journey, then the distance may seem very long and difficult. If you enjoy your walk, then you will be in the moment while you are walking, and your destination will appear when you are ready to be there."

I have a feeling that he's talking about more than the distance to the meadow here, but I'm not ready to go there. Yet. I get his point, and that's enough for now. "Okay, Clarence, I understand. And, since I'm enjoying the walk, the meadow may be just ahead, but we aren't there yet."

He smiles and begins to walk again. I stand for a moment, looking at my field. I try to see the ocean as he's described it, but I really can't. I accept the fact that he views the sea, and that's really all that's necessary I guess. I can imagine the sea, but I actually see the mustard fields. Maybe there isn't any difference between imagining and seeing. What if I walk into the field, imagining that I'm wading in water? Will my feet get wet? I'm just about to test that idea when I hear Wee Bet's voice. Perhaps another moment.

Reunion and a Question

*Each visit gives me opportunities to welcome
knowledge as a guest.*

"Well, Ardeth, shall we walk together like old times? It's so good to see you again." Bet has dropped back to wait for me, and when I look away from my field she stands at my side and Clarence continues on ahead of us.

I take her arm and we begin to walk together. "So, you remember too? I can't recall the place, though. Can you?"

"I think so, but the picture is fuzzy. We were friends, but you lived on Crete, and I was in Egypt, studying to be a priest. I suppose it was a pretty unconventional friendship."

I'm beginning to remember a bit. "Yes, I think I recall a little of it. I wonder why I seem to forget? So many lessons learned, and each time I approach the visits with new eyes."

"I know, Ardeth. I feel as though I keep learning the same lessons over and over too. I suppose that's because we don't always understand when we experience things at first. All in our own time, as Clarence would say. I have to keep reminding myself of that, but there always seems to be so much to do, and

I want to get on with it. I get impatient with myself because I'm always in such a hurry."

"I feel that way sometimes too, Wee Bet, but maybe it's just a matter of understanding. I know I choose my own lessons, for reasons that aren't always apparent to me at the time. Each visit gives me opportunities to welcome knowledge as a guest, but I just wish it didn't always seem as though I were greeting this guest for the first time. Perhaps we'll walk together again somewhere. A review of old lessons wouldn't be a bad idea."

"I'd really like that. Maybe when the time comes Clarence will help. But now, I have a question for him. Let's catch up." She gives me a generous hug, and we hurry on to join Clarence.

When we reach him, Bet asks her question. "Clarence, I want to ask you about our conversation back in your office. I think I understand your story about the two friends on the road, but I just want to be sure that you were answering my question. You know, about helping people."

Clarence nods and lightly touches her arm, indicating that he wants her to look down the lane ahead of us. I expect to see the rest of our group as I look too, but I guess they're either behind us or way ahead of us because I certainly don't see anyone familiar.

THE POOL

Having healing hands only means that you can help.

Five people are walking toward us. They're a motley crew to be sure, and none of them look well at all. A very old woman, ancient really, is wheezing and coughing as she struggles to walk. Each step is difficult for her, and every time she coughs, her gnarled hands come up to clutch her chest. Her lips are dry and cracked, and she keeps licking them to find some bit of moisture that might have strayed from her mouth. She's assisted by a younger woman who is almost bent double. The younger woman walks as though her knees hurt with every step she takes. The women are accompanied by two men; a man with only one leg is supporting himself with a crutch while he leans on another man whose right arm is missing. And finally, there's a frail young boy who walks very slowly. I haven't ever seen any of these people before.

As the strangers approach us I notice that there's a clear pool of water just along the side of the lane to our left. I look from the pool to the group coming toward us and think they all look so tired and thirsty a cool drink might be welcome.

65

Wee Bet and Clarence must feel concern for the weary travelers too because all three of us quickly move over to the water, indicating to the strangers that we'd like them to join us.

I walk over to the very old woman and help her to the pool. As she bends over to drink, I hold her so she won't fall. While the woman drinks, I look into the water. I can see her reflection, but I can't believe what I'm seeing. The reflected image is that of someone who is young, strong, and beautiful. The old woman sees the reflection too because she immediately straightens up and shouts, "Look! Look at me! I've never seen myself like this before." Before I can comment, she runs off dancing and singing. Amazing.

While I stand there trying to understand what I've just seen, Bet moves over to the other woman and helps her at the pool. The young woman's knees creak as she bends over; I can hear them as Bet helps her get a drink. As I watch the two of them I can tell that this woman sees her reflection too, and judging from her reaction, she's surprised at what she sees. I move closer so that I can see too. This woman also sees a healthy, young woman, but she looks at the reflection in disbelief. "That isn't me. I have sore feet and my knees hurt. Help me up. I don't want to be here." Wee Bet looks as though she wants to say something, but instead she reluctantly helps her up, and the woman limps away.

Now both Wee Bet and I are staring, first at the pool and then at the woman who has just left us. The old woman is nowhere to be seen. This is very strange.

Wee Bet is shaking her head. "What's going on here? Why did they leave so quickly, and why did they both react so differently? And why didn't their reflections match their real images? I'm confused."

I'm about to add my confusion to Wee Bet's, but I notice that the man with one arm is moving toward the pool, and I want to watch him as he bends over to drink. He too sees his reflection, which reveals a healthy man with two strong arms. Before I know it the man is bouncing a ball that's just suddenly materialized, and while I stare, he tosses the ball through a hoop that somehow has miraculously appeared in the limb of a tree. He keeps throwing the ball through the hoop, over and over again, until I call to him and ask him what he's doing. It looks to me like he's playing basketball, but I want to hear his version of this strange exercise.

"I'm practicing. I've got to practice so I can get ready to have fun."

Practice? Get ready for what? I don't have time to do anything more than gape before I see that Bet has joined the man with one leg and is helping him to the water. He also sees the reflection of someone strong and healthy, with two good legs, but he shakes his head. "No, this is not God's will.

God's will is to suffer. I will be led by the Right One when the time comes. He'll tell me." He then hobbles away, still on one leg, supported only by his crutch. The basketball player is gone too. This is very strange indeed.

I turn to ask Clarence what's going on, but he's busy helping the frail young boy to the pool. As they bend over so the boy can drink, the young boy's eyes become wide and shining. "Look! I see my grandma. Isn't it wonderful? I'm going to see her soon, I know. I'm so happy."

"We will rest here awhile, then, laddie. Come and sit." Clarence speaks gently as he leads the boy to the grass near the side of the pool.

As I watch them, the woman with the creaky knees appears again and hesitantly comes back to the pool. She looks puzzled. Wee Bet is there immediately to help her, and when she looks into the pool, the woman again sees a beautiful, healthy reflection. She turns to Bet. "Can that be me? No, it's you! I see you. But maybe I can be well too because I see your reflection." This time, when she stands, the woman is young and strong. She points to Bet and begins to shout. "You have healing hands! You have made me well! You have the power!"

Now it's Wee Bet's turn to look puzzled. She looks from the woman to Clarence, a question beginning to form in her mind. "Clarence, is it...?"

"Nay, Wee Bet. It is not you. But if this woman has gained confidence, you can lead her back to the pool so she can see that it is her own reflection, not yours, which she sees. If you do not do this, she will become nothing more than a servant to you. If you ask her to find your socks or suspenders (I have to suppress a smile here because I have a hard time visualizing Wee Bet wearing socks or suspenders), she will want to know what color they are, where you have put them last, and if you want them now. She will depend on you for direction. Having healing hands only means that you can help, but you must lead her back to the pool so she can see that the reflection is her own. She must see herself. She must not be dependent on you."

At that moment, without any warning, all five strangers move toward Clarence, and the young boy, who is no longer frail and weak, speaks to him. "If you have no further need of us, we'd like to continue with our lessons."

Clarence nods, thanks them, and they all walk away. Strong. Healthy. Perfectly well.

We watch them go, and I turn to Clarence. "I get it. It was a set up! You arranged to have them here."

Clarence just smiles and looks over at Bet, who stands so still she hardly seems to be breathing. "Do you still have a question, lass?"

I don't think Bet trusts herself to speak at this moment, so she just shakes her head. No. No questions.

This is turning out to be a most enlightening walk. Not only is it a really sparkling day, but I'm able to be with such interesting people. I wonder if I can have a word with Ho Yung. I want to find out if he remembers me too.

Apparently my thoughts are pretty obvious, because as I look around for him, he comes up behind me and touches my arm.

Ho Yung and Ardeth

Remember the lessons learned, not the events themselves.

"Ho Yung, when we were back in Clarence's office, as I looked at you, I kept seeing flames and...please don't laugh... sheep. Any idea what that might mean?"

He looks at me intently, and as I return his gaze, he begins to change. The man becomes a young girl. A brown-haired, peasant girl without shoes. Helena. This is Helena. Now I understand why Mother Superior saw Elizabeth when she looked at me. That's how she knew me, and that's how she saw me.

Helena smiles and takes my hand. When she touches my hand I begin to cry. Our time together comes back in a rush of anguish and guilt as tears drip down my face. There's no stopping them; I'm overcome with sadness. I saved her life on a visit, and she tried to return the honor by protecting me for as long as she could. Balance. I'd taken the papers, and the soldiers were after me. She wouldn't tell them where I was, so she was burned at the stake like so many others. I can see the flames again. The innocent little girl who loved her sheep and never

71

meant to hurt anyone gave up her life to save mine. And for what? I too was burned because eventually they found me. The memories flood over me, and I'm overwhelmed.

"Elizabeth. Ardeth. No, please. It is not necessary to feel guilt. My choices were there too. You were not responsible. We are each responsible for ourselves. You know that, and so do I. Do not open old wounds because of a memory. Remember the lessons learned, not the events themselves. Did you not hear what Clarence said to Consuela? If you continue to cling to people and events, their significance for you is lost. I admit that I left cursing you and your god, but my last visit, and the solitude that I chose, helped me to understand that. Often a visit provides a means to understand the lessons chosen in a different life. By gaining a new perspective it is possible to learn within a different setting."

As I listen to her words, I gradually gain control. The image of Helena fades, and once again I see the one I know now as Ho Yung. "Thank you, my friend. For more than you know. I sincerely hope our paths will cross again. Perhaps on my next visit that will be possible."

He smiles. "Yes, I think we can learn much from one another. The world I have chosen will be very different for me, and a friend will be most welcome."

"I welcome the opportunity to learn with you, Ho Yung. Perhaps you might even be willing to help me with the book

I want to write?"

"Yes, of course. It would be my pleasure."

BEAUTY IN THE MEADOW

Beauty is the ability to see. That is the miracle.

I look ahead and see that the lane leads into a huge meadow. I guess it's time to be there. Tall grass and flowers become more and more visible as we approach the meadow, and what appeared to be a blur of color from a distance now takes on vibrant detail as we come closer.

"Clarence! Everybody! I'm over here follow the path to your left."

We can hear her, but the grass is so tall it's hard to see, so we just follow the path as she suggests. It's Dorothy, of course.

The voice is unmistakable. We continue our march, single file like little children on an adventure with their teacher. Why not? As we walk down the path, we can hear a steady stream of chatter – rather like verbal popcorn – that guides us to our destination.

Soon we come upon a small clearing and there she is, down on her hands and knees, staring intently at a very strange looking flower.

"Come and see this have you ever seen a checkered flower with such a delicately formed blossom a work of art truly a work of art!"

Her enthusiasm is contagious, and soon we're all gathered around her, admiring the little flower that has captured her attention.

"That's the most curious thing I've ever seen. Looks like a little bell." Louise has edged her way to the center of the group and is down on her knees with Dorothy. "What's it called?"

"*Fritillaria lanceolata.*"

"A what?" Now Arturo moves closer.

"It's a checker lily belonging to the *Liliaceae* or lily family."

"What an unbelievable name. It sounds like something one might wear or eat. It doesn't look real. How could those checks be natural? They look painted." By now Thomas has moved in closer to inspect the greenish-yellow flower with the purple checks.

I'm sure we must look like an odd group. We're all bent over, inspecting a single tiny flower as if we've never seen one before. Even Clarence is studying it. Well, I suppose it would be more accurate to say that we haven't seen a flower quite like this one before.

I feel very content to be with these people in this place. Somehow, who we are doesn't matter at this moment. It only seems important that we're all entranced by the beauty of one fragile flower.

"Lads. Lassies. Can any one of you tell me what beauty is?"

Clarence has stepped back and is watching us. He's heard my thoughts again. He often does that, although he never really intrudes. He only verbalizes someone else's thoughts if the subject is one to be shared because he intuitively knows the difference between private, personal thoughts that are meant to be kept that way and thoughts which are speculative in nature. Once again we all start talking at the same time.

"Beauty is understanding the wonder of existence."

"I don't agree. I think that some of the greatest beauty in life lies in the mystery that defies understanding or explanation."

"That's true, but I think mostly that beauty is happiness and being with someone you love."

"I think it's more than that. Beauty is knowing. Beauty is order and symmetry in an intelligent universe."

"Beauty is enjoying the wholeness of life and the thrill of helping someone see her own reflection in the pool."

"I'd have to say that beauty is something I've built that I'm proud of. It's craftsmanship."

"Beauty is growing things watching them grow the miracles of nature everything about life is beautiful."

"You're all so…so…abstract! Not everything is beautiful. I've seen some really ugly things in my times. Depends on what's important to you. Beauty can be anything you want it to be."

By the time everyone has offered definitions and comments, we're all seated on the ground again, gathered in a circle, surrounding the flower that's been the focus of our attention. Except Clarence. He isn't sitting because I don't think his girth would allow him to be very comfortable on the ground. As I look up at him, I wonder if I should offer to get his blue chair.

"You almost have it. Your thoughts flow with a very similar rhythm. You all knew it as you looked at Dorothy's flower when we first arrived here. You felt it then. Beauty is the ability to see. That is the miracle."

We're all silent as we absorb what Clarence has just said. So simple and so right. The ability to see. I know he isn't just talking about the physical act of looking with our eyes. Without the ability to see there would be…nothing. The simplicity of the statement is…beautiful.

Just then our reverie is interrupted by the laughter of children, and we all stand up and look in the direction of the sounds.

ANIMAL MESSENGERS

We go back, again and again, because we're messengers

Not too far away, I see two men standing near horses. There are four small children nearby. A dark-haired man is stroking a golden-colored horse while a black stallion nuzzles his shoulder. The other man, fair haired, stands staring off in the direction of the sun. One small boy sits atop the palomino, and a girl with shiny black hair fashioned in pig-tails is braiding the horse's tail. Two other children appear to be trying to get something out of the dark-haired man's pocket. Just off to the side of the black horse three small silver-gray dogs sit attentively, ears cocked, heads tilted to one side. Listening and watching. As the one child produces what appears to be an apple out of the dark haired man's pocket, one of the dogs, slightly larger than the other two, wags his tail in approval. I can't help but feel that if I were in the dog's position I might wish for a cookie instead of an apple, but I suppose some dogs enjoy fruit too.

"Who are they, Clarence?" Wee Bet has to stand on her toes in order to see, and she asks the question.

"The one stroking the horse is Joseph. He takes care of the animals and teaches the children to care for them as he does. He teaches the children many things. He is about to take a journey too, so he is saying his farewells...for now."

As Clarence is identifying the one nearest the horses, the other man begins to walk away from the group. He's heading toward the sun, and as we watch him, he seems to disappear from sight. We all see him because when he separates himself from his friends it's enough of a distraction to draw our attention.

"Where did he go?"

"Who was he?"

"How did he just disappear?"

Wee Bet, Consuela and Louise all have questions.

"I do not know his name, but he has gone to another place. He has work to do elsewhere."

"Horses and dogs! We don't need more animals. The world is overpopulated already, and now even here we have horses and dogs. Ridiculous. And look at how those children and that man talk to them. Absurd. Why waste time talking to animals? They can't understand you."

The words just shoot out of his mouth and cut the serenity of the moment in half. Thomas is being insufferable again.

Clarence responds very calmly. "Thomas, why do you think animals can not understand you?"

"Why? I think that's fairly obvious. Because they're not human. They don't have the ability to think and reason. I've never seen a logical animal. They operate totally on instinct."

"Aye. And you think understanding is a matter of thought, reason and logic?"

"Of course. How else can you understand something unless you think it through or reason it out? Intelligence makes understanding possible. Only those who are capable of reasoning can achieve any degree of understanding. And, as far as animals go...."

"You pompous twit! What the bloody blue blazes gives you the right to make a statement like that? *Understanding is a matter of logic.* That's the most foolish thing I've ever heard. What about intuition and feelings? What about love?" Louise has come over to Thomas and is standing about two inches away from him, jabbing at him with her finger as she speaks. Her face is red and she's shouting. "Self-righteous bigot! You really are such a dolt."

"Love? What does love have to do with understanding? It isn't even related. And it certainly has nothing to do with animals. I...."

"Thomas." Clarence interrupts him. He's calm but firm. "We will talk again. Alone. Between now and then, if you will please think of these things: knowledge, learning, intuition, and instinct. Your thinking will help us when we speak again."

"Of course, but I think...."

"We will talk later."

That's as close to a dismissal as I've ever heard from Clarence. I'm glad that he's stopped Thomas from saying anything else because at that moment I want to punch Thomas in the nose. Just one solid hit would make me feel so good. What an ass. Never mind; let it go.

I decide that I'd better move away from Thomas before I say or do anything I might regret later, so I walk over to the three small dogs and greet them.

"Hi, you three. How're you doing this beautiful day?"

All three dogs move closer to me as I bend down to run my hands over their shiny, soft hair. I sit down so I can touch all of them, and as soon as I'm settled they all crawl into my lap.

"We're fine, Ardeth. And, how are you?" The spokesdog for the group looks up at me and smiles.

"I'm good. What's your name, my friend, and how do you know my name?"

"My name is Tuppence, and these are my friends, Duncan and Duffy. We know your name because we're going to join you on your next visit. Don't you know that?"

"No, I don't. How do you know?"

"Because I can see all of us together in what you would call your mind's eye. Other dogs will join you too, but we'll be your first animal family."

I'm fascinated. "That's wonderful, but how do you know we'll be together? I don't know it; how can you?"

By now the other humans except Thomas, who's probably off sulking somewhere, have joined me and are listening to my conversation with the dogs. No one looks as though they understand Tuppence's comment any more than I do. Good. At least I'm not the only one who is confused. Clarence just stands there and smiles. He smiles more than anyone I've ever met.

"Clarence, how can the dogs know what I don't know?

"Lassie, listen to the wee lass. Let her tell you."

Tuppence leans against Clarence's leg and looks up at me.

"Ardeth, in this place, where we are now, there is no time. Do you understand that?"

"Yes, Tuppence. I know that."

"Good. Because there is no time, all of our lives are here for us to see. When I look at you and see into your heart, I see us together. It's simple."

"I understand and accept what you see, but I don't understand why I don't see it. Why don't I recognize the three of you as being a part of my next visit? Seems like I should know that on some level."

Clarence interrupts at this point with a question. "Ardeth, allow me ask you this. When you saw the dogs, what were you feeling?"

"Well, when I first saw them, I was drawn to them, but before I could feel much of anything, Thomas started his rant about animals. I felt so angry with him that I wasn't feeling anything else."

"Aye, just so. You were angry, and that anger contaminated every other feeling you might have had. You lost your ability to see."

I'm back in the molasses again, this time with my foot in my mouth. "Okay, I understand. But once I came over to talk with the dogs, I forgot about Thomas and just enjoyed being with them. Why didn't I see our connection then?"

Tuppence comes over to me and puts her two front legs up against my knees, indicating that she wants me to pick her up. I reach down and scoop her up into my arms and hold her close. She whispers in my ear. "Use your intuition, Ardeth.

Don't try to analyze. Just be. You're thinking so hard about your next visit you aren't seeing clearly. Relax. Just know that we'll be together."

The others don't hear what Tuppence is saying to me, but I must be smiling, because they all smile too, and the momentary tension is lifted. I'm about to ask another question, but Arturo speaks up before I can begin.

"You know, Clarence, seeing these three dogs here makes me wonder. Surely there must be other animals here besides the dogs and those horses we saw. Where are they?"

"Do you need to see them, Arturo?"

"Well, yes. I guess that I do."

Clarence nods to Tuppence and she returns his nod with one of her own. While we all watch the two of them something really incredible happens. I mean really incredible. The three dogs multiply. I don't mean that they split apart, but one moment there's just the three of them, and then there are more...and more...and more...until there are so many animals all around us that I can't even begin to count them. Dogs, cats, birds, horses, snakes, every imaginable kind of animal all blend together in a whirlpool of energy. If this extraordinary image were a picture in a book, I might call it a collage, but this mélange is three-dimensional.

We all stand with our mouths open, trying to take in what we're seeing. Except Clarence, of course. He just smiles again.

"Lads. Lassies. What you are seeing is what you might call a Collective Unconscious made visible by your desire to learn. When animals come here their energies become part of the Collective. If they experienced a difficult visit, the hardships they endured are absorbed into the Collective and balanced by the positive energy of those who had a pleasant journey. Some stay for what you would see as a long time, while others travel again.

"Do they choose, just like we do, Clarence?" Wee Bet asks what I'm thinking.

"Nay, lass. They simply respond to the vibrational frequency they hear from humans who desire their presence."

Louise is pacing. "But with all of the cruelty and abuse that goes on with animals, why would they continue to make visits? People aren't always kind to animals, and I would think if they had a bad time they'd just stay here where they could be part of the Collective, as you call it. Why go back again?"

One small dog separates herself from the whirling energy mass and stands in front of Louise. "Louise, hello. My name is Cinny. I can answer your question. We go back, again and again, because we're messengers."

Louise smiles at Cinny and bends down to hug her. "All right, little one, tell me this. Who are you bringing a message to?"

"To humans, of course."

"Just exactly what message are you bringing us?"

Cinny grins at her and looks at the other animals that are still swirling around us. "Why don't I let them tell you? Listen carefully."

Surrounded by this fantastic display of animal energy, we hear a chorus of voices. The animals all seem to be speaking as one, yet individual voices can be heard.

"Love without limits."

"How to use your intuition."

"Live in the moment."

"Acceptance without judgment."

"All life is valuable."

"Death is only physical change."

"Peaceful coexistence."

"We're all one."

I'm sure there are more replies to Louise's question, but these few stand out like solos among the chorus of voices. As we're serenaded by the animal choir we all begin to smile and nod with more understanding than I would have given us credit for a few moments ago. When the animals see us smile and nod, the collage flattens out, dissipates, and soon we're left with just Tuppence, Duncan and Duffy.

"Arturo, have you had your question answered?" Clarence stands with the three dogs and looks at Arturo, and then at each one of us.

"Yes, Clarence. I certainly have. Astonishing. I had no idea."

"Tuppence, will you talk with us a bit about the message of peaceful coexistence? I know what it means from a human point of view, and I also know that we don't do it very well, but I'd like to hear about it from an animal's perspective." Wee Bet bends down in front of the three dogs as she asks her question.

"Certainly, Wee Bet, but I know a being that could give you an answer from personal experience. Would you like to meet Lakota, the wolf?"

"Oh yes, I really would. Where is he?"

The answer to Wee Bet's question materializes in front of us as she speaks. Not only do we see one wolf, but an entire pack stands patiently waiting for us to acknowledge them.

One wolf separates himself from the group and walks over to Tuppence. The wolf lowers his head so that he and Tuppence are standing, nose to nose, and a whispered conversation occurs between dog and wolf that we can't hear. The other wolves seem to be able to hear them though, because they all move closer to the one talking to Tuppence. After a bit, Tuppence makes her introductions. "Everyone, this is Lakota and his family. I think Lakota can answer your question by telling you about himself."

Lakota, now surrounded by his pack, begins to tell us his story. "Hello. It's good to meet all of you. As Tuppence said, this is my family. I just came Home to be with them again, and

I can tell you that it's wonderful for all of us to be together. We've been separated for many earth years. When I was very young, my family and I were resting by a stream one day when all of a sudden humans came after us. I had to watch while the hunters killed my family, and then they threw a big net over me and took me away. I was moved from one zoo to another until finally a humane society rescued me, and I lived in a quiet place until my body died and I came Home. People there cared for and about me, but I was no longer free and I had lost my family. For us, and all animals that were made to live free in their natural habitats, peaceful coexistence means allowing us to be what we are. It means respecting our rights to live freely in our own places. We are all one, and we must live peacefully with each other to maintain our very essence. Does that answer your question?"

Wee Bet nods, moves over to Lakota and puts her hand on his head. She turns to look at the rest of us and, as one, we all join her, each of us reaching out to touch this beautiful animal. As we stand there feeling his thick coat, the other wolves come closer and form a circle around us. We feel their energy and their love fills our spirits.

I don't know how long we stay together but the moment, or however long it is, is so profound I'm moved to tears. Soon we're all crying. We cry for the cruelty that humans have inflicted on these marvelous animals. We cry for Lakota, especially, because he was a prisoner. And, we cry because we feel their happiness in being together.

After awhile, Lakota gently leans against Wee Bet. "Thank you for being with us and for giving me the opportunity to tell my story. Now we must go, but if you listen closely you will be able to hear our song in the wind."

And then they're gone. Another lesson learned.

A part of me wishes that Thomas had stayed with the group because we've just had an awesome experience, and he's missed it. But since he doesn't believe in talking to animals, there's hardly any point in his being here right now. He doesn't believe animals can communicate; his belief system controls his understanding, and he'd probably say that we're hallucinating or something. Still, I feel sorry for him because he's missed seeing the animals and hearing what they have to say.

Clarence walks over to me and shakes his head. "Nay, Ardeth. You can not judge. Did you not hear the animals? Thomas is allowed to be who he is, just as we all are. His lessons are not the same as yours. Do not be arrogant."

"Arrogant? Me? That word would be better used to describe Thomas, don't you think? How am I arrogant?" My blood pressure is soaring again.

"Lassie. Lassie. When you feel sorry for someone because they do not share your beliefs you establish yourself as being superior to them. You can not do that. Leave this be. Think about what the animals have told you. Remember their messages."

At this point the three dogs move toward me and stand in front of me in a group-expectant pose. They don't say anything; they just look at me. Without judgment. I feel only love from them as I absorb their energy and relax. My, oh my, do I have a lot to learn.

"We'll see you soon, Ardeth. Be well. We'll come when we feel your energy." All three smile as they say their good-byes, and then they're gone.

As much as I really don't want to acknowledge it, seeing the dogs leave triggers a slight sense of urgency in me. It's almost time for me to go too. I try not to think about the headache, because I'm actually looking forward to the visit. I haven't ever been to Chicago...and I want to see those dogs again.

"Well, Clarence, I think it's time for me to be getting to the Park. I'll be leaving soon. It was good to see all of you, and I hope we meet again." I feel sad.

"Aye, lassie, but you need not walk alone. We can go to the Park with you. Those who will be leaving shortly can stay with you until the time comes, and the rest of us will not be far away."

"Good. I could use the company and moral support."

We find our way out of the meadow and back to the lane, this time led by Dorothy, who knows a short cut. Once on the lane we continue our little parade toward the Park. I haven't ever approached it from this direction before, but I can see the great wheel in the distance, so I know we're going the right way.

I walk very slowly, and the others, bless their hearts, adjust their pace to mine. They know I'm reluctant to leave, and they want to stay with me, no matter how long it takes us to reach the Park. Very considerate friends.

As we walk, I think about my next visit, trying to put my lessons in some kind of order. The rest of the group senses that I need some alone time, and they talk quietly among themselves as we walk. I'm lost in my thoughts when I hear a shout that startles me so much that I almost jump straight up in the air.

THE TRAIN

Greed provides a bandage for a wounded soul, but the wound will not heal if it is never exposed to the light.

"Hey! People! Get out of my way!"

A very loud noise that sounds, unbelievably, like a train whistle punctuates the shout that precedes it. "Move over. You're on the tracks!"

Tracks? We aren't walking on any tracks. But we all do respond immediately, regardless of where we think we're standing. As the whistle becomes louder and more insistent we move quickly to avoid whatever or whoever is chasing us.

As we stand off to the side of what we thought was a lane, but now looks like tracks, a train lumbers past us. An old-fashioned, steam-billowing, whistle-blowing locomotive. The engine is bright red and the cars are each painted a different color. What is this? Some kind of circus train?

While we stand to the side of the tracks trying to catch our collective breaths, Dorothy starts to shout. "Stop! Stop! I want to ride the train c'mon everyone let's catch the train."

Before any of us can respond, Dorothy runs after the train. Fortunately it isn't going very fast, and before long we can see that she's caught up to the locomotive and is yelling at the engineer, or whoever it is that's operating the train. We can't hear her very clearly, but whatever it is she's saying must be making an impression because the train gradually slows and then stops.

Eager for another adventure, we all hurry to catch up to Dorothy to find out what we have here. It's obvious that we're seeing a train, but where has it come from? Why is it here? Where's it going? Too many questions. Be in the moment, Ardeth.

When we reach Dorothy, we can see that she's engaged in an animated conversation with the person who is driving the train. Driving? Does one drive a train? Whatever. A man with bushy hair sticking out under his engineer's cap is leaning out the window of the cab. He's only visible from the waist up, but I can see the straps of what no doubt are bib overalls, and he has a red bandanna tied around his neck. Well, he certainly looks like an engineer.

"Lady, I just told you that you can't ride the train. You don't have a ticket, and besides I'm in a hurry. I only stopped because I thought you needed help."

"I have their tickets, sir. Please allow these people to board." Clarence, now miraculously dressed in a conductor's uniform, moves to the front of the group, holding tickets in his hand.

We all stare at Clarence, and then look up at the engineer who's looking at his watch, shaking his head.

"Okay. Okay. So, you've got tickets. Big deal. But you still can't come with me. I don't have any room."

"What do you mean you don't have any room?" Louise looks down the track at the ten cars that are attached to the locomotive. "Looks like you've got plenty of room to me. You're pulling ten cars."

"No. No. You don't understand. The cars are all full. No room for people. I've got to go." The engineer's face is red, and the veins in his neck stand out as he sputters at Louise.

Without saying another word, Clarence walks over to the door of the locomotive and motions us to follow him. The engineer glares at him, but there's something about the determined way Clarence moves that stops him from saying anything else. Instead of speaking, the engineer quickly runs to the door and jumps down to the ground before any of us can move to follow Clarence.

The engineer's blue striped bib overalls look new and don't seem to have any of the grease and dirt on them that I expect to see. He wears a white shirt under the overalls, and it too is spotlessly clean. What he's wearing seems more like a costume than actual working clothes. I'm even more curious as I look at his hands and see that they too are clean and don't appear to be the hands of a working man at all. And, he wears rings on every finger. Why would a train engineer be wearing so many rings? The man is a walking contradiction.

Now his face is really red, and perspiration coats his fore-
head as he shouts. "No. No. You can't get on the train. This is
my train, and I don't have any room. I keep telling you that."

We all step back, but Clarence isn't bothered a bit by the
shouting as he points to the rest of the cars. "There is no need
to shout. We have tickets and we would like to ride your train.
Please show us to a car that will accommodate us."

Not to be outdone by Clarence, Thomas, who has joined
us again, pushes past us to get to the engineer and stands nose
to nose with him. "See here, my good man. We have tickets.
We will ride this train. Kindly show us to our seats."

"I told you. There's no room. You're not listening. What
else do you want me to say?"

"Well, then, buster, we'll just ride up front with you."
Louise to the rescue.

"Lady, you can't ride with me. It's too dangerous. There's
no place for you to sit, and I can't be responsible if you fall and
hurt yourself. Please, just go away. Find another train. Just
leave me alone. I'm late already."

"I want to see the other cars. I don't believe that you don't
have room." Arturo is adamant as he starts to move toward the
first car. We all follow, but the engineer moves faster than we
do, and by the time we get to the door of the car he's blocking
it with his body. What's up with this man? Why is he being
so stubborn and unreasonable?

"Just what is it that you're hiding, sir? Why won't you at least let us see what takes up so much room in ten cars that you can't allow us to ride?" Ho Yung speaks quietly, but he's hit right on what it is about this man's attitude that bothers me. He does act as though he's hiding something. All of his posturing isn't a natural response to the situation at all. After all, we're just curious. What harm is there in indulging our inquisitiveness?

When Ho Yung asks his question the man seems to deflate a bit. Now he looks worried, and he speaks defensively. "Hiding? I'm not hiding anything. Everything on this train is mine, and I'm going to see that it stays that way. Just remember that. But I'm not going to argue with you any more. Go ahead and look if you want. Just don't touch anything. I need everything that's there. It's all mine. Hurry up and look because I'm late."

With that, the engineer stands aside and allows us to board the first car. I don't really know what I'm expecting, but I'm certainly not prepared for what I see.

All of the seats have been removed, and the car is filled, floor to ceiling, with furniture. Chairs, couches, tables, beds, desks, and cabinets are randomly stacked on both sides of the car. A narrow aisle down the center allows us to walk single file through the car.

No one says a word. There doesn't seem to be an appropriate response to this car full of household furnishings, so we just keep walking. When we get to the end of the car, Clarence, who is in the lead, opens the door that leads to the next car.

This car is filled with all kinds of appliances; refrigerators, ovens, washers, and dryers are all stacked on top of each other just as the furniture is in the previous car. Again, a narrow aisle offers a way for us to get from one end of the car to the other.

"Is this guy some kind of one man moving company? What is all this stuff?" Louise is as confused as I am. I can't figure it out either.

Now that we've started our parade through this moving warehouse, we just keep going, curious to see what we'll find in the next car...and the next....

The pattern soon becomes clear. Each car holds different contents, and by the time we've worked our way through the last car we've seen not only furniture and appliances, but food, jewelry, clothes, toys, electronic equipment, works of art, musical instruments, and books.

Once we've walked through the last car we all exit and step down to the ground. The engineer is impatiently waiting for us. He's obviously been pacing as we've taken our tour because he's worn a path in the dirt next to the tracks. "Okay. You all satisfied now? I told you there's no room. Tickets or not, you can't go with me." He starts to walk away.

I take his arm, just to get him to stop so we can talk, and before I know it I find myself flat on my back. He's done some sort of really fast move on me that I didn't see coming at all. I'm more surprised than hurt, so I quickly get to my feet and dust myself off before anyone can worry about me.

Immediately I see that I shouldn't be concerned about the group worrying about me because when I look around I see that they've surrounded the engineer, and Arturo and Thomas are holding him still. They aren't worried; they're angry.

"Nay. Nay, lads. There is no need to respond in this way. Give the man room, and he will answer your questions. Is that not correct, lad?" Clarence has walked over to Thomas and Arturo and has removed their arms from the now panicky engineer.

"Sure. Sure. Whatever you say. I just don't like anyone to touch me." He turns to me. "Sorry about that. Didn't mean to hurt you, lady."

I smile and tell him that I'm fine. I also apologize for taking his arm. I'm feeling awfully polite for somebody who's just been knocked down, but I do realize that I shouldn't have grabbed his arm.

Finally we all sort ourselves out and the questions begin. In varying tones of incredulity, curiosity and accusation, we all ask him the obvious questions. His responses are brief, but even when we've completed our inquisition I really don't feel any more enlightened than I did before our question and answer session. Something's missing from this picture.

Wee Bet tries to summarize what we've learned. "All right, then, sir. If I understand you correctly, the contents of this train belong to you. Everything. You rent the train from a traveling circus. You have an apparently unlimited supply of money to purchase these items. You're bringing what you have here to a warehouse, which contains more of the same. You make these trips on a regular basis. You never sell any of these goods, yet you never really use all of them either. You spend your energy accumulating possessions. Do I have it right?"

"Yeah, I guess, but when you say it that way it doesn't sound like much. These things are very important to me; I need them. Can't you understand that?" The engineer is so uncomfortable with this line of questioning he's almost whining in his desire to be understood.

Consuela looks at him and shakes her head. "No, I don't understand why you need all of these things. If you can't possibly use everything you gather, why do you keep collecting?"

No response. The engineer just looks at her as if she has two heads. Now he's confused.

Clarence comes to his rescue with a response that says it all. "Because, lass, this is who he is. His possessions identify him. He does not wish to be valued for himself; thus, he surrounds himself with material goods. Is that not clear?"

Ho Yung interrupts before Consuela can respond. "Why not share what you have, sir? There are many who could benefit from what you have gathered."

"Share? You gotta be kidding. Why would I share? Everybody else can take care of themselves. This stuff is mine. Mine."

Clarence turns and motions for us to follow him. "Come, lads and lassies. The man needs to continue his journey, as we do ours. Leave him be. He has answered your questions. You simply need to accept what he has told you."

Clearly understanding that he's been dismissed, the engineer runs to the locomotive, climbs up, the whistle sounds, and he's on his way. The train and all of its contents rumbles past us and soon becomes a smaller version of itself in the distance. Moments later the train is no longer visible and neither are the tracks. We're back on the lane.

"All right, Clarence. What was that all about? I know there must be a lesson involved. Please clarify." Thomas, for once, has the same question I think we all must have about what we've seen.

Clarence, now dressed as he had been before we'd encountered the train, smiles and nods. "Aye, lad. There is a lesson here, as there is with all human behavior. What do you think it is?"

Thomas rolls his eyes. "I don't know. That's why I'm asking you. The man is obviously driven to accumulate possessions. I have no idea why."

"I wonder if he has a wife and children." Wee Bet is thinking out loud. "I should have asked him that. Do you suppose he gathers people as he does material goods?"

"Perhaps, lass. Let us ask him." Clarence turns, and suddenly the engineer is standing in front of us, bewildered and anxious.

"Hey! What am I doing here? I need to be back on the train."

"Aye, lad. But the lass here has one more important question for you. If you will please answer her you may resume your journey."

"Okay, what's the question? Make it fast."

Wee Bet smiles at the engineer. "I was just wondering if you have a wife. And children. Do you have many children? What about other family members? Brothers? Sisters? Are there many other people in your life?"

"Not that it's any of your business, but maybe if I answer your foolish questions you'll leave me alone. I've had many wives. And children. Those too. I gave them everything they could ever want, but eventually they all left me. Or, sometimes I left them. Now it's just me. That's the way I like it. Satisfied?" He turns to Clarence. "May I go now? I really need to get back to my train. Someone might come along and steal my possessions. I have to be very careful."

Clarence nods, the man disappears, and we're left to deal with more unsatisfactory answers. None of us can seem to get a handle on what this is all about.

"I get it! I get it!" Louise looks like a schoolgirl who's just come up with the right answer to a difficult question. "It's all about greed, isn't it Clarence? What we've just seen is the price somebody pays for being greedy."

"Yes, of course. That must be it." Consuela stares at Clarence expectantly. "He needs his possessions because he's afraid that people won't accept him for who he is. The people in his life have left him because he can't, or won't, give them his heart."

Ho Yung responds thoughtfully. "This way of life of his is very safe, is it not? Relating to people, interacting, demands personal scrutiny. It is much easier to surround oneself with external validation than to search one's soul for identity. Greed provides a bandage for a wounded soul, but the wound will not heal if it is never exposed to the light. This man never allows light into his life. He lives in the darkness of his own over-crowded shelter. He is hiding. He is safe from scrutiny."

Clarence nods and looks at the rest of us to see how we're dealing with what Ho Yung and Consuela have said. We all nod too. I'm about to make some sort of comment about how sad it is that someone would choose to live such a life, but before I speak I remember Clarence's caution about judgment and remain silent. I'm learning.

We continue to walk, and I think we're all clear about what we've seen and learned until Wee Bet speaks up and asks a question we probably all should have thought to ask.

"Clarence, I understand what we've seen, but what I don't understand is why we're seeing it here? Home is a place for reflection and evaluation. Surely he knows that he doesn't need his possessions here?"

"Aye, lassie, but often those who return Home bring their previous needs with them. It takes a bit of reflection for them to realize that the visit and all it meant to them was just an illusion offering a way to learn. When that realization becomes reality for our engineer friend he will rid himself of his possessions."

"But how's he going to do that? What will happen to all of that stuff?" Louise is being very pragmatic as usual.

Clarence smiles and points toward a large mountain that looms in the distance. I don't think any of us realize that we've been walking toward a mountain, but we've been preoccupied with the train and probably haven't noticed it. Or, perhaps we haven't needed to see it until now. In any case, there it is.

"If we walk a bit faster and you look very carefully you will be able to see the answer to your question, lass." As Clarence talks he steps up the pace, and we all hurry to stay with him.

As we move closer to the mountain I can see train tracks winding their way up and around the mountain, a bit like ribbon encircling a large bushy rock.

"Look! There's the train. He's on his way to the top of the mountain." Consuela directs our attention to the train we now all see in the distance.

Steam billows from the top of the locomotive as the train slowly winds its way on the tracks that snake their way to the top of the mountain. Even though it isn't a direct climb, the grade is steep, and the train struggles to keep moving. I feel like I'm watching a re-enactment of the story about the little engine that could, but I don't believe it can this time. Finally, the train slows and wheezes to a stop.

As we watch we can see the engineer hop down from the locomotive. He stands and looks at the ten cars for a moment, shakes his head, and then quickly runs back to the last car and opens the side panel. He scurries around for a bit, removing items from the tenth car and placing them in the ninth car. This goes on until he's loaded the ninth car so full that he can't close the door. It isn't possible for him to transfer all of the items from the tenth car to the ninth car, and so, with great reluctance it seems, he unhooks the tenth car and leaves it sitting there while he walks back to the locomotive. He climbs up, and we can see the train begin to move again. Very slowly. Now he only pulls nine cars.

The absence of one of the cars seems to help for a while, but soon the train falters again and stops. Still pulling too much weight.

The engineer doesn't appear for the longest time, but I know we'll see him sooner or later. Sure enough, he hops down and walks back to the ninth car. We watch as he repeats the process he's gone through with the tenth car. Now there are eight. I try to put myself in his place and can only imagine how difficult it must be for him to leave so many of his precious possessions behind, but he's doing it.

The locomotive has an easier time towing only eight cars, but the grade becomes steeper as the train climbs, and I know it will only be a matter of time (so to speak) before he'll have to unload more cars. True enough.

"Poor guy. He's going to have to leave everything behind."
Louise is amazingly sympathetic, considering the fact that
earlier she'd thought the engineer to be so foolish."

"Is that not the point, lass?"

Yes, indeed, that's exactly the point. We're watching the
shedding of a skin that is no longer needed. The engineer is
releasing his greed in order to get to the top of the mountain.
I wonder if, at some point, he'll try to back down the tracks,
thinking that perhaps his possessions are more important than
the journey.

But he doesn't. We watch him reorganize, load, and then
uncouple every single car as he labors his way up the mountain.
It's an exhausting process, and even though we aren't close
enough to see, I know that his overalls and white shirt aren't
clean any longer. He's probably sweaty and dirty. Getting rid
of excess baggage is hard work.

After what seems like a very long time, only the locomotive
can be seen scaling the steep mountain. I think for sure he'll
make it to the top now that he isn't pulling any cars, but
eventually the locomotive falters and comes to a grinding stop.
One last burst of steam escapes from the smokestack and all
is quiet. Now what?

We all hold our collective breaths as we wait to see what the
engineer will do. I know what I hope he'll do, but he's been so
determined I'm not sure what his next move will be.

Finally the man emerges from the locomotive. He slowly
walks down the steps and slumps down on the bottom step.

Clearly, his energy is depleted.

Wee Bet takes Clarence's arm. "Do you think we should go up there and talk to him? He must be exhausted and depressed. Maybe we can help."

"Nay, lassie. He will be fine. He needs to think his thoughts and make his own decision. Just watch. You will see."

I'm thinking that the engineer is going to sit there forever, but finally he stands up, pats the locomotive, and starts to walk up the mountain. I'm surprised to see that he isn't carrying anything because it seems reasonable that he would try to carry a few of his possessions with him, but he walks empty handed. And, interestingly enough, as he walks his heavy steps become lighter, and he walks faster and faster. He seems rejuvenated and energized. Eventually he begins to run, and soon we lose sight of him as he nears the top of the mountain.

I feel like cheering. Yes!

Clarence puts his arm around Wee Bet's shoulders and smiles at her. "Have you seen the answer to your question, lassie?"

She smiles in return. "Yes, Clarence, I certainly have. What a wonderful sight to see him running like that. It was quite a struggle, but he made it."

"His stuff! What happened to the train and all of his possessions? Everything's gone. It's all gone!" Louise is shouting and pointing to the now empty track.

"Aye, lass. He does not have need for those things any longer. He knows that now. His warehouse no longer exists either.

The manifestation of his greed has vanished with his need. Now he will be free to reflect on what he has learned so he will be able to continue his journey. Are there other questions?"

No one speaks. Enough has been said, and the lesson has been taught. No further need for commentary.

We continue our walk, all silent in our own processing of the information we've been presented. My, my.

The Balloonist

He must untangle his own knot.
Then perhaps he will learn to weave.

As I look ahead I can see a very large white and silver balloon. The shimmering ball floats rather haphazardly, like a huge bubble with strings that seem to be pulling it slowly to the ground. The closer we get the larger it becomes, and by the time we've walked a bit farther the balloon has landed. We see a man trying to untangle the mass of strings that has collapsed around and on top of him. They aren't really strings though; once we're close enough to distinguish size more clearly the strings can be seen as a heavy network of ropes that connects the balloon to a basket that was once suspended beneath the balloon, but now has settled in a crumpled heap on the ground. Not a very successful landing.

The balloon has descended right in the middle of the lane, and we all gather around and begin to help the man untangle himself from the ropes and mass of material. The steady hissing of air confirms the fact that there's a puncture in the fabric, which has caused the balloon to gradually deflate and fall.

We have a marvelous time trying to separate the man from the ropes and heavy material; at one point we're all tangled up, trying to help him get loose. A litter of kittens with a ball of yarn, scrambling on and over each other.

Finally we manage to set him free, and he emerges tousled, but unhurt. He's disgusted and angry.

"I knew something would go wrong. I knew it. Finally, finally I get a perfect day for flying, and look what happens. I've worked for ages to make the right adjustments, and now look at it. Look at it. Destroyed. Kaput. And all because of a small tear that I never noticed when I was doing my pre-flight check. The higher I flew, the bigger it got, and finally, well… you can see what happened."

He shakes his head and starts to rummage through the material, looking for the source of the hissing air that still can be heard quite distinctly.

"Are you all right did you hurt yourself maybe you should sit down here let me help you." Dorothy has gone over to him and is trying to get his attention.

The man is half buried underneath a maze of silver at this point, and all we hear is a muffled growl. "No. No. You've helped me enough already; it's hopelessly tangled now. Just leave me alone, and I'll get this blasted thing fixed and try it again."

Dorothy gets the message and backs away. We all look at Clarence to see if he's going to say anything to the balloonist, but he just shrugs his shoulders and continues to walk. The man doesn't seem to want or need our company any longer, so we edge around the collapsed balloon and leave him to his troubles.

Before we've walked too much farther, Consuela comes up to Clarence. She's concerned. "Why didn't you talk to him or offer to help him? I was surprised that you just left him there. We could have helped. You could have helped."

Good questions. I think we're all a little taken aback because Clarence seems to have just dismissed the man.

Clarence knows Consuela is asking for all of us, so he stops walking. "Lads. Lassies. It is important that you learn to ravel before you tie up in the skein. You need to be able to untangle the knot, and then to also weave. Not the one without the other."

"What's this ravel and skein business, Clarence? We're not talking about knitting. I don't get it." Louise speaks up right away on that one.

"Nay, but can you see the sense in helping the man when he does not ask for help and feels he needs to make repairs himself?"

"Clarence, really. It's obvious that he got himself into his present situation, but it certainly wouldn't hurt to offer him some assistance." Thomas, the humanitarian, has spoken. "Aye, Thomas, we could offer him further assistance, but the problem is his, and he wishes to solve it himself. We will not always be there to help. He must untangle his own knot. Then perhaps he will learn to weave."

Ah ha. Touché, Clarence.

We continue on our way without any more questions. I look back once to see how the balloonist is coming along, and I see him untangling ropes and spreading the balloon material on the ground. He must have found the tear and is ready to repair it.

I hope he knows how to weave.

SECOND THOUGHTS

...sometimes is it not also true that the importance of
the lessons can only be seen in the light of the
new experience?

I feel more and more reluctant to leave. These are nice people, and I'm having a good time. It would be so easy to just stay and be with them for a while longer. Perhaps I could even contact my nurse again and see how she's doing. I stop walking as these thoughts wander through my head and see that Clarence is standing beside me.

"What is troubling you, Ardeth? Are you having second thoughts?"

"I don't know. I suppose. It's just that it's so...easy and peaceful here."

"Then why do you not stay?"

"Because I need to leave. I have things to do that I can't really do here because the opportunities aren't the same. For the lessons I've chosen this time, I need to be somewhere else. I just wish each visit weren't quite so much like starting over again. I always forget and have to cover the same ground again and again."

"Aye, lassie, that may be true, but then sometimes is it not also true that the importance of the lessons can only be seen in the light of the new experience? You still are who you are, even though you look in the mirror with new eyes and the reflection appears to be different. Change does not occur unless you wish to make it so."

"I know, Clarence. I just wish I knew all of me a little better."

"Well, then you best be getting on with your lessons."

Louise and Consuela come up just then, in time to hear the last part of our conversation, and Louise has a question. "What if she changes her mind, Clarence? What if she's on her way and has second thoughts? What then? I know how it is once you're in that Chute. It's hard to stop once you get going."

Good question, Louise. Very good question.

"Aye, lassie. It may be hard to stop, but anything can be changed. If she changes her mind, she will simply come Home. That can be done any time. Everything is changeable."

Well, that's a relief. Who said you can't go home again?

We're getting closer. The fields on either side of the lane have been replaced by rolling hills. Or have they? Well, whatever. I see rolling hills now. I turn to ask Clarence what he sees, but he's dropped back to talk with Dorothy so I keep walking. The rest of the group stays slightly behind. They want to give me time to think. Well, I've done that, and now it's time to see. To be somewhere else.

THE AMUSEMENT
PARK

ROUND AND ROUND

Each visit is not better or worse than the previous one;
it is just different.

The great wheel towers up ahead. Even from a distance I feel dizzy looking at the giant spoked circle as it spins round and round. Up close everything else seems dwarfed by the size of this enormous contraption.

When we arrive at the entrance to the Park a large iron gate stands open, and we just walk through. No admission charge.

Free. I have to smile at that one. Sure, it's free all right. Why wouldn't it be?

Once inside the Park we're assailed by a cacophony of sounds and smells: calliope music, rattles, clangs, chattering voices, running feet, popcorn...hot dogs. I feel like I'm being swallowed up whole. No. Not yet; not yet.

"C'mon, Ardeth, don't look so serious. Let's go for a ride!" Louise grabs my hand and starts to pull me toward the giant Ferris wheel. "Everybody! Hurry up! It's stopped now, and we can just make the next ride."

I have absolutely no desire to fly around in that thing, but Louise's enthusiasm is really hard to resist, so before I know it we're seated and ready to go. There are twelve seats on the wheel; each is completely enclosed and has a cage in front for protection. We aren't strapped in, but a bar holds us in place. I don't relish the thought of going around and around at all, and when I realize that the seat is mounted in such a way that we'll be upside down as we get close to the top, I'm even more reluctant.

I start to get out. "Enjoy yourself, Louise. I'll wait for you on solid ground. You can tell me all about it. This does not look like fun."

Too late. I barely finish my protest when the motor starts up and we're off. I'm dizzy already and we've hardly moved.

Round and round, upside down, downside up, round and round. I hate it, but Louise is having a wonderful time.

The motion doesn't bother her at all. In fact, she's actually laughing. I can hardly breathe, and I begin to feel nauseous.

All of a sudden we stop. Instant relief. I'm half way out of my seat and in the process of unhooking the bar when I realize that one more step will send me off into the air. We aren't near the ground. Not even close. The fool thing has stalled, and we're suspended, almost upside down, somewhere up near the top. Terrific.

"Now what? Why have we stopped here?" I want to get off. Right now.

"Relax, Ardeth. Don't be so nervous. They're probably just loading more passengers."

"Relax? You must be kidding. How can I relax while I'm suspended, practically upside down, in mid-air? What if the seat comes loose? What if the cage breaks?"

"Don't be dull. Nothing's going to happen. We'll be going in a minute."

Easy for her to say; she isn't miserable. At this moment I think about all of the advantages of being a bird. At least a bird is in charge of its own flight, not an unwilling passenger in a cage suspended from a motorized circle operated by some incompetent dolt.

"But Clarence, there must be a progression involved. Each visit has to be an improvement over the previous one."

That's Arturo's voice. I lean forward a bit, (a very little bit) and look through the wire mesh. Sure enough, Clarence and Arturo are in the seat ahead of us, which puts them at the very top of the wheel. Their car is hanging completely upside down. How can they possibly be carrying on a conversation in that position? I decide to listen, figuring that at least my eavesdropping will provide a distraction. Anything to keep my mind off the fact that we're stuck in a cage that isn't moving.

"Arturo, look where we are. Tell me what you see."

"Where we are? Do you mean right now, Clarence?"

"Aye."

"We're riding the wheel, and we've stopped to load more passengers. I can't see very much right now because we're upside down."

"Are you in a better position than anyone else on the wheel just because you are higher in the air and at the top of the circle?"

"Better? No, I suppose not. It's just a different position. We're all riding the wheel."

"Aye, lad. Exactly. We are all riding on the wheel. Expand that thought. Each visit is not better or worse than the previous one; it is just different. Just as what you see from this position is not better or worse than what you would see if you were sitting in a seat ahead or behind the one you are in now. All of the seats go around. There is no ladder to climb with a prize at the top. Think of a circle, not a straight line."

"But Clarence, what's the point of the circle if you don't get anywhere?"

"Why did you get on the wheel in the first place, my friend?"

"To go for a ride, of course."

"And have you ridden the wheel before?"

"Yes, many times."

"Has each ride been exactly the same for you, then?"

"No, the kind of ride I have depends on what my mood is, what kind of a day it is, and who I'm with. It depends on many things, but I'm not sure I follow you."

"All right then, lad. Think about what you have said. Each time you ride you go in a circle. No matter where you sit you still move in a circle. One seat does not have an advantage over any other. Yet, you say the ride is not always the same for you. I think you could look at those elements which make the ride different each time and answer your own question."

"Fine, Clarence, but I'd rather climb a ladder. At least when I get to the top, I know I've arrived somewhere."

"Tell me then, Arturo, when you build a house, do you put the roof on last?"

"No, the roof goes on as soon as the house is framed in and is able to support it. You need the roof to make the wall framing secure and for protection from the weather when you move inside to do the interior and finish work."

"I see. Yet, the roof is the highest point of your house, and you would need the very tallest ladder you have to reach the roof. But when you finish the roof there is more to be done.

You must climb down the ladder and build other parts of the house. And, then perhaps you will climb back up again. Up and down. Up and down. What is the difference, lad, if you go up and down or around and around?"

"Maybe there's no difference, but aren't some visits more important than others, Clarence?"

"Is the roof to your house more important than the walls, the windows, or the foundation?"

"Well, the roof may not be more important, but a house wouldn't be complete without a roof."

"Aye, complete you say. Laddie, a circle is very complete, is it not? And when the ride on the wheel is over, you can choose to ride again if you like. Or, you can choose to not ride at all. Enjoy the ride, Arturo. The prize may be the experience itself."

I'm about to respond to Clarence's last comment, since I figure that if I can hear them they're able to hear me, but before I get a chance to say anything the motor starts and we're off again. Wonderful. Maybe the infernal thing will stop at the bottom and let us off.

Finally the wheel does slow down, and the ground becomes a very welcome friend as it comes up to meet us. When we do stop I can't get out of the seat fast enough. I stagger away just in time too because I hear Louise calling after me. Something about another ride. No thanks; enough is enough.

MADAM ZOLOFF

There isn't any past, present or future.
There are just experiences.

I walk quickly, and I do mean quickly, away from the wheel. My head is clearing, and I figure if I can get far enough away so that I can't hear Louise calling me I won't have to endure another ride on that infernal machine. I look back, just once, but I think I'm safe because I can see Louise and Dorothy getting on the wheel. Good. Dorothy will have a great time, and I can continue my walk up the Midway.

As I absorb the sights and sounds, my attention is drawn to a tent just ahead on the left side of the midway. The tent itself is multi-colored, and there are all kinds of astrological symbols painted on the tent fabric along both sides of the opening. Just above the entrance is a sign that reads "Madam Zoloff – Fortune Teller."

I stop just long enough to get a closer look at the various symbols, and as I'm studying them I hear a voice calling from the inside of the tent.

"You there. Come in here. You need your fortune told."

I look around to see if the person speaking is talking to me, or perhaps someone else, but there's no one in front of the tent except me. I guess she's talking to me.

"Don't just stand there. Get in here."

Oh, well. Why not? I walk through the tent opening and find myself in an enclosed area that smells of incense. There isn't much light, but I can see a woman seated at a small round table. The tasseled cloth that covers the table is worn, and predictably, a large crystal ball rests on the table, as well as a deck of oversized cards. Large pieces of silk and satin in various shades of purple are draped all over the interior sides of the tent, and the ground is mostly covered with deep red carpeting. The carpet is a bit faded, like the tablecloth, but the combination of purple on the walls and red on the floor still creates a feeling of opulence. The atmosphere is exactly what one would expect in a fortune teller's tent.

"Don't just stand there. Come and sit down."

I can see now that the disembodied voice I heard when I was outside belongs to the old woman seated at the table. She motions for me to come closer, so I walk over to her and sit in the empty chair she's pointing to on the other side of the table. A green scarf hides most of her gray hair, and large gold hoop earrings dangle from her ears. Her dress is many layers of vibrantly colored silk and satin, just like the walls, and assorted silver and gold bracelets cover her arms. She looks just like a gypsy.

"So, Ardeth, what do you want to know?" Her smile reveals stained teeth, some of which are missing. Not an unpleasant sight, really. Just completes the slightly tattered look of her.

"How do you know my name?"

Her answer is accompanied by a laugh and another smile. "Sweetie, why wouldn't I know your name? I'm a fortune teller, after all. And that's not all I know about you." As she talks, her hands are constantly moving, caressing the crystal ball, shuffling the cards.

"Sweetie." Not a word typically used to address me, but I like it; it's kind of nice, actually. I hesitate a bit before I respond to her statement about knowing more about me than my name because I'm not sure that I want to hear what she has to say. I've entered the tent and it's probably too late to make an exit, but I feel a bit uneasy even though I'm too curious to leave now.

"What else do you know about me, Madam Zoloff? That is your name, isn't it? I saw it on the sign outside."

"Yes, indeedy, that's my name. Pretty classy, isn't it?"

I don't know if it's a classy name or not, so I just smile and nod. I think she's teasing me a bit

"Well, then, let's see. I know that you're about to leave us to go on a visit. I know that you aren't really anxious to go, but you feel you have to leave here in order to learn whatever it is you've decided you want to learn. I know that you're going to a place called Chicago to take care of some people in return for the loyalty they showed you when you were a pompous ass in the Canary Islands. I know...I know you really don't want to hear any of this. Shall I go on?"

"No. Yes. I don't know. You're right about everything you've said, but I'm not sure I want to hear about my future. Maybe I'd be better off just doing it and not knowing anything about it before I go."

Her restless hands spread the huge cards, fan-like, on the table. "Here. Pick a card."

I choose the card closest to me, and when she turns it over I see that the picture is of two fat cherubs holding up a large globe. "The Universe" is written at the bottom of the card.

"I see. Very interesting." She makes no further comment.

"What's interesting? What does it mean?"

"What it means, Ardeth, my sweet, is that the whole universe is available to you. Something is ending and beginning at the same time. But then, you already know that. You have many options open to you. Many choices. You know that too. Pick another card."

I'm not sure I know everything she thinks I do, but I pick another card as she requests. This time the card I draw has a picture of a skeleton with the word DEATH written at the bottom of the card. I'm a bit startled by the graphic image.

"Oh, lordy, Ardeth. Come on, don't look so spooked. Death is only change. You know that too. Why do you suppose you drew that card?" She sits back and waits for my answer.

"Well, I guess it's because I'm about to make a change. A big change. But does the fact that I drew the death card mean that the change is going to be negative?"

"No, silly girl. It just means change. Don't get all riled up about the picture. It's just a symbol. Here, look into the ball. Tell me what you see."

I do as she asks, and I see many people, all of whom seem to look like me, doing a variety of activities in several different settings. Some of the people are men; others are women. The styles of clothing worn seem to indicate that the people live in different time periods. "What am I seeing here? Are these people all me?"

"Of course. You're seeing yourself experience many lives in various and sundry places. What do you think it means?"

"Well, since this is a crystal ball, I guess I'm seeing my past, present and future, all magnified in the ball." I haven't a clue, really, but this is the first thought that comes to mind.

"Not bad. Not bad. But look here; look at this one." She points to the me who's walking on a path near a body of water. He's wearing a robe and sandals, and he's carrying some kind of clay tablet. "What if you wanted to be this man again? What if you wanted to understand something that you might have missed during this visit? Do you think you could revisit?"

"Revisit? I'm not sure I understand what you mean. If this image represents my past, then I would have to say no because

I've already done that. I think I lived on Crete at the time, during the Minoan period. If what I'm seeing represents my future...well, I guess it doesn't, because you said revisit."

Madam Zoloff gives a disgusted sigh and shakes her head. I've obviously displeased her, but I don't know why. "Why are you shaking your head like that?"

"Ardeth. Ardeth. How long have you been here?"

"How long? I don't know. There isn't any time here. Surely, you know that."

"I do, but you seem to have forgotten. Perhaps you haven't lost the imprint from your last visit, and you're still thinking about time in linear terms. You can't do that. It doesn't work that way. There isn't any past, present or future. There are just experiences. What you're seeing in the ball is simply all of you. You can visit any experience you wish, at any time, so to speak. Do you understand what I'm telling you?"

"I hear your words, and to some degree I do understand. But it's so hard not to think in terms of time. I guess maybe I haven't been here long enough to lose that need to measure experiences using time as a frame of reference. Let me ask you this. What about reincarnation? What do you think of that idea? Maybe that's what you're talking about."

She laughs and begins to shuffle the cards again. "What a strange concept. Why do people always have to have such names that conjure up so many misconceptions? Humans create the concept of linear time, and then they bind themselves to it. There are no re-incarnations. There are only incarnations.

You can be born in as many bodies as you like, but there is no time frame to bind you. All life happens simultaneously. You simply pick and choose which incarnation you wish to experience. Here, let me show you."

As I watch her, Madam gets up and begins to pull several books from an open cabinet that sits in the back of the tent. I hadn't noticed it before, but now I see that the shelves in the cabinet are crammed full of all kinds of books. She moves back to the table, places the crystal ball and the cards on the floor, and proceeds to lay out six books. She then randomly opens each book in front of me. After all of the books are opened, she sits again. "All right, dearie, tell me what you see here."

I wonder if this is some kind of trick question. What I see is obvious, but maybe not. She reminds me a lot of Clarence. "Well, I see six books in front of me. They're all open to different pages."

"Good. At least there's no problem with your vision. Now, read the books."

"Read them? All of them? Right now?"

"Just do as I say, Ardeth. Pick up a book and read the page you see in front of you. Then, pick up another book and do the same thing. Do that with all of the books. Can you do that?"

"Yes, Madam. I can do that." I don't tell her that I think this is really a strange way to read books. I think her request is quite odd, but then she is too I guess. The request is consistent with the person making it, and I do as she asks. When I've finished reading from each of the books, I sit back and look at her. "Okay. I've read the pages in front of me. Now what?"

"What do you think? Don't you have any idea what we're doing here? Don't you understand how what you just did relates to my answer to your question?"

At this point I've forgotten the question, as well as her answer to it, so I just shake my head. I don't want to tell her that I don't remember, but judging from the way she's looking at me, she knows.

Another sigh. "The question, sweetie, had to do with reincarnation. I was telling you that there isn't really any such thing. I told you that you pick and choose lives that you wish to experience. Like you just did with the books. Imagine that each book is a life you wish to experience. The books are all there in front of you, just as your lives are. When you read one book, you're consciously experiencing that life. Then, when you want to read another book, you pick that one. And so on. Do you get it now?"

"I think so. So, you're saying that my lives, like the books here, are all there in front of me. They all exist simultaneously. But I can't consciously experience all of them simultaneously, so when I'm consciously living one life the others are still there, but they're in, maybe they're in my subconscious mind. And, I can go back and forth, from book to book, from life to life, as many times as I want to. Is that what you mean? Is that what you meant about revisiting the experience in Crete?"

"Now, you're getting it. The time thingie really makes humans think there's only one way to move, and that's not true at all. Forget about time; it only gets in the way."

"You know, Madam, I'm thinking that what you've just said explains something I experience now and then that I call bleed-through, and I wonder if I'm right. Sometimes I have an image of what could be me in another life, right when I'm experiencing a life that has nothing to do with what I see in my head. It feels like a memory, but I know that most times we think of memories as remembrances of the past. I guess I could have a memory of a so called future life too, couldn't I?"

"Bleed-through. I like that. Yes, indeedy, my sweet girl. You don't shut yourself off completely from all of your lives just because you're experiencing one particular one. Sometimes you might need a little bleed-through to remind you that you're more than one person. To remind you that you have lifetimes of experience you can draw on when you need to do that."

As she talks, Madam Zoloff removes the books and places them on the floor. She then lifts up the crystal ball and cards and arranges them back on the table. When I look into the ball, I see the same images of me that I'd seen before, but now I'm looking at them with different eyes. When that realization registers with me the images in the ball fade, and I only see a warm, yellow light saturating the inside of the ball.

"So, sweet Ardeth, do you wish to know about your future?"

I smile at her and shake my head. "What future? There's no such thing, Madam. Surely you must know that."

Now she laughs and reaches over to grab my hands in hers. Her hands are rough, but they're warm and strong. "Be gone with you then, my sweet friend. Enjoy your visit. Read your book. Learn your lessons. Come back and see me when you return, and we'll talk."

I stand and offer to help her replace the books on the shelves, but she just waves me away and mutters something about other customers needing to read too, and not to bother. I thank her for what she's taught me and walk back out to the Midway. I have a lot to think about.

And, as usual, I have more questions than answers.

RING AROUND THE BOTTLE

...there is no such thing as just cause and effect. There is always direction. Choice.

The sunlight dazzles; I guess I didn't realize how dark it was in the tent. I can see that only a few people are at the Park right now, which is fine with me. I'm not a great one for crowds, and I'm happy to be able to walk down the Midway without being crushed in the masses that often gather. People are coming and going all the time, and it's usually a busy place.

135

Popcorn. That's what I need. Maybe that will help to ward off the headache. Nothing like popcorn at the Park. It just doesn't taste the same anywhere else. Wonder why that is? Another lesson. Even the culinary ones often seem to be mysterious.

I find a vendor and satisfy my urge with a large bag of popcorn. Butter dribbles down my chin as I walk along, happily munching. There are sideshows on both sides of the Midway, and the barkers are all competing for everyone's attention as they shout their invitations:

"SteprightupfolkssteprightupseetheamazingAnidashe dancesshesingssheswallowsfiredon'tmissityou'veneverseen anythinglikeit!"

"Knock the cans over. Anyone can do it!"

"Pitch pennies and win a prize!"

"How's your aim? Hit the target and win!"

"Throw the rings!"

"Hey, Miss. Can you help me get up here?"

A little guy, really short, is trying to throw rings around the bottles, but he can't see over the counter. A definite disadvantage. "Sure. Here, hold my popcorn, and I'll lift you up."

I set the boy on the counter and stand behind him as he begins to throw the rings. One after another, each ring he throws lands neatly around a bottle. He never misses. With my bag of popcorn still in one hand, he uses his other hand to pick up a ring, throw it, and then pick up another.

"Here, Miss. You can have your popcorn back now."

"That's okay, you can finish it if you'd like. May I throw some rings too?"

He smiles, starts to eat some popcorn, and hands me a few rings to throw. "Sure, help yourself."

I take the rings, look carefully at the bottles stacked at the back of the booth, and start to throw. I miss every one of them. The boy hands me three more rings. Once again, I aim, throw, and miss. This goes on for several minutes until finally I stop. "I guess I'm no good at this. Here, you go ahead and throw the rest."

I hand over the remaining rings on the counter and watch as the boy throws each one around a bottle. Again, he never misses.

"How do you do that?" Seems like he should occasionally miss, and I should be able to hit at least one.

"What?"

"You never miss. How do you make the ring go around the bottle each time you throw? I can't even get one to land in the right place."

He's finally run out of rings, and he turns to look at me. "Oh, that's easy. There's nuthin' to it."

"Easy for you, maybe, but I can't do it. What's your secret?"

"No secret. I just see 'em there. That's all."

"What do you mean you just *see* them there? I don't understand what you're saying."

"Well, uh, I don't exactly know how to explain it. Lemme see. Before I throw, I close my eyes a second and see the ring around the bottle. Then, I just make it happen. It's kinda already done when I really throw the ring, so it always lands where I see it."

"Wait a minute. Let me see if I understand what you're saying. You're telling me that you see the ring around the bottle in your head before you throw, and that makes it possible for the ring to land in the right place?"

He smiles. "Yeah, that's it. I make my arm throw the ring where I see it. No big deal, right?"

"Well, maybe not to you. But what if your aim is off?"

He's puzzled. "Why would my aim be off? My arm throws the ring where I tell it to. I told you that. Why're you making this so hard? Here. Do it again."

As he's talking, the boy hops off the counter and lands inside of the booth. He reaches down, comes up with a handful of rings, and gives them to me. "Okay, just do what I did. Close your eyes. See the ring around the bottle. Just throw it where you see it."

I take the rings, close my eyes, see the ring around the bottle, open my eyes, and throw. Another miss. I try again. The ring misses again. "I can't do it. Why isn't it working for me?"

"I dunno. Did you think it was gonna work?"

"Well, sure. I guess. It worked for you, didn't it?"

"Yeah, but did you really believe it was gonna work for you? I bet you didn't. You just did it the way I said, but you didn't really think it would work."

"Aye, lassie. He's right you know." I turn to see Clarence standing behind me. He reaches around me, picks up a ring, and throws it perfectly around a bottle. The ring never even touches the sides of the bottle as it settles around the base.

This is too much. Impatiently, I grab another ring, close my eyes, see the ring around the bottle, throw, and miss one more time. Then another. And another. The rubber rings thunk the bottles, never once circling them. The bottles never fall over, because I guess they're glued in place, but by the time I've finished my furious display of incompetence not one of my rings has found its way around a bottle.

"Lassie. Stop. Think about what you are doing. Or, about what you are not doing. Why do you think you are not able to do this exercise?"

"Yeah, Miss Lassie. Why can't you do this? What's the matter with you? I told you how to do it."

"All right, you two. Wait a minute. Let me think this through. I know you showed me. I did just what you said to do, and it didn't work."

"Aye, Ardeth. But was the wee laddie correct when he said that perhaps you did not believe it would work? Is that the problem?"

"I don't think so. I saw him do it, so I knew it could be done. You just did it yourself. Of course, I believed him. Why wouldn't I?"

"I do not know, lassie, but you did not make it happen as he did. Perhaps he can show you again, only this time, if he would be so kind as to talk to you while he is doing the exercise you may be able to understand."

The boy rolls his eyes, shrugs his shoulders, and reaches out his arms so I can put him back up on the counter. Once there, he turns to me. "Okay, Miss. One more time. Listen up. I got the ring in my hand. I'm closing my eyes. I'm seeing the ring around the bottle. I'm opening my eyes. I'm telling my arm to throw the ring around the bottle. There. It's done."

Another perfect throw.

"Wait a minute. You didn't tell me that you told your arm to throw the ring around the bottle. You said that you just saw it there, and your arm threw it in the right place." I'm sputtering.

"Lassie. Lassie. What are you thinking? Do you really believe that the body responds automatically to what is seen? It is true that body and mind work in concert, but there is no such thing as just cause and effect. There is always direction. Choice."

I feel myself stepping out of the molasses, one sticky step at a time. "Clarence, are you saying that because I didn't actually direct my arm to follow what I saw in my head, that it didn't happen automatically?"

"Aye, Ardeth. Go on."

"And...and...the ring didn't land where I saw it in my head because I didn't make it happen. I just expected it to happen."

"Geeze, Miss Ardeth, I told you when we first started that I made it happen, but I guess you didn't hear me. It's kinda like you took yourself outta the loop. Here, try again. Only this time, do it right. I'm gonna need another bag of popcorn if we stay here much longer."

I take the ring the boy hands me, close my eyes, see the ring around the bottle, open my eyes, tell my arm to throw it there, and...I do it! I grab more rings and repeat the exercise, over and over. Every ring lands around a bottle.

Clarence and the boy applaud, while I furiously throw rings. Now I'm having fun. Finally, when there are no more rings in sight, I stop and smile. "Where's my prize?"

The boy jumps off the counter, lands on the inside of the booth, and grabs a stuffed teddy bear. "Here, Miss Hot Shot. You sure earned this. I gotta go now. See ya later."

As the boy runs off through a side entrance to the booth, I turn to Clarence. "Another lesson, Clarence? Was this a set-up too, like the people at the pool?"

"Nay, lassie. This was just an opportunity to learn. You did well."

"Thanks, but let me ask you this. When you were talking about cause and effect, were you saying that there's really no such thing because before there's any cause there's always choice? And, before there's any effect, there's also choice? Is it kind of like: choice-cause-choice-effect?"

"Aye, lassie. That is exactly what I am saying. Everything is a matter of choice. Even the simple act of throwing rings around bottles. You must choose to make it so."

"I think I get what you're saying. So, out of my frustration about throwing the rings comes a lesson. And, I've even won a prize for learning it. Nice."

"Aye, Ardeth. There is always a prize for learning, even though it may not be as tangible as the wee bear you now hold. I can see that you are warming to your lessons. Hold these thoughts on your visit; you will have need of them."

I'm about to ask what he means when I hear a scream.

CHAMBER OF HORRORS

Fear masks our ability to see who we are.

I turn to ask Clarence if he's heard the scream too, but he's wandered off somewhere. He's always doing that. Hit and run lessons. As I stand there trying to figure out if I've really heard the scream I hear another one. This one is so chilling that I actually stop breathing for a moment. I look around for the source of what certainly must be some kind of disaster, but nothing seems to be wrong. Others walking along the Midway must be hearing the screams too because anxious looks are exchanged, but I can't see people running anywhere. I continue to walk and hear more screaming again. This time I hear several screams and a few moans. There definitely has to be something awful happening somewhere.

Still clutching my teddy bear, I look around and then realize where I am. I'm standing directly in front of the Chamber of Horrors. The screaming and moaning are coming from inside. What a relief. The sound effects are so realistic they really had me going there for a minute.

I look toward the opening, which is constructed like the mouth of a cave, and see huge spikes sticking out from the edges of the aperture. The sides and top of the arch are ringed with chains, whips and weapons. Very effective. As I'm admiring the potency of the set, a man and a woman emerge from the opening.

The sunlight must be a drastic change from the interior of the chamber because the people are blinking and rubbing their eyes. I haven't ever gone through it, and since I'm curious, I take a moment to talk with them. Maybe they'll tell me what it's like.

"Did you folks have fun?"

The woman replies first. "Fun? Well, I don't know if you could call it that, exactly. It was frightening."

"I'll say." Her partner doesn't look very enthusiastic either. "I didn't care for it at all."

I'm a little confused. They really look awful, so it couldn't have been a very pleasant experience for them. Their faces are gray. "Why would you subject yourselves to something so horrible?"

The man speaks up. "Oh, I don't know. She wanted to go. I did too, I guess."

I turn to the woman. "Why did you want to go? I'd like to understand."

"Because I've never done that before. I wanted to know what it was like, but I've done it now, and I won't feel a need to go through it again."

"I understand about needing to have new experiences, but what you both went through was obviously very difficult. Would you mind telling me what you felt you needed to do?"

The woman holds the man's arm and looks up at him. "You tell her. I'm not sure I'm ready to talk about it yet."

Nodding, the man begins to talk. "Well, we both wanted to experience fear. We wanted to know what it felt like to be afraid and to understand what fear was all about, so we visited a place that allowed us an opportunity to do that. We were black-skinned people. Slaves. Other people who were not of our color treated us badly, and eventually they killed our bodies because we tried to run away. They caught us and shot us. We returned Home. End of story."

"I'm sure it wasn't as simple as that, was it? Did you understand why the people treated you badly?"

The woman answers. "No, not at the time. We couldn't figure it out then, but I think I'm beginning to understand now. They were afraid of us because we were different. They didn't know what to do with their fear, so they used it as a weapon. They wanted to control us because we weren't like them. We were afraid too, not because we were different, but because they beat us and treated us badly. We were not only afraid for our lives, but we felt fearful because we didn't understand. Isn't that ironic?"

I don't get her point. "Ironic? In what way?"

"I see now that fear shows itself in many different ways. When we were in that place I thought we were the only ones who were afraid. I didn't see that those who mistreated us were afraid too. I wonder if it would have made a difference if we'd known that."

I shake my head. "I don't know, but it sounds as though you learned something really important. You learned that fear contaminates and also that it wears many different faces. Understanding how fear motivates people is a good lesson, I think. Don't you?"

The woman seems about to answer my question when I see her smile, and before I can respond, she and her companion quickly walk around me. When I turn to see what's captured their attention I see Clarence and the rest of the group standing behind me. I have no idea how long they've been there, but judging from Clarence's greeting to the couple, they've heard our whole conversation.

"Lassie. Lad. It is good to see you again. In listening to your talk with Ardeth I see that you are understanding much about the fear you have experienced. And you, Ardeth, are learning as well."

"Have any of you had a visit like ours?" The man places his arm protectively around the woman as he asks his question.

Louise speaks up first. "I have, only my experience with fear was different than yours. It was more about how I felt about myself than other people. I was afraid to follow my heart; I kept trying to please everybody else. I thought that if other people liked me and approved of me, then I was a worthwhile person. I let others define who I was. Big lesson for me. I don't need to do that again."

Wee Bet nods. "I've done that too, Louise. Only I think my most important visit about fear was when I was afraid to be healthy. I was sick all the time with one illness after another. Finally, my poor body just couldn't take any more abuse and I returned Home. I didn't understand until I got here that I was hiding in my illnesses because I was afraid to be well and take responsibility for my life. Being an invalid gave me an opportunity to demand that others take care of me. I always seemed to find people who needed to do that, mostly so they wouldn't have to care about themselves. That visit wasn't much fun at all."

"I was afraid to love anybody. I had a visit where I was a woman who went from one partner to another, looking for someone to love, but I was always afraid that I'd never find anyone. I know now that I was afraid that if I loved someone that person would hurt me in some way. Soon it became easier not to allow myself to love at all. It was a pretty safe way to live, but it wasn't a very enjoyable visit. I didn't understand that I was responsible for my own feelings and that I needed to feel hurt so I could avoid making any kind of commitment. Each time I felt hurt I wore that pain like a medal." Arturo takes a deep breath and shakes his head. "When I first came Home I thought it had been a wasted visit, but now I know better."

Thomas clears his throat. Now, this might be really interesting. What kind of fearful visit could this annoying man have had? I'm prepared for a lecture, but instead his comments stop my judgmental little mind in its tracks. "I was afraid to…to…try anything new. I know that doesn't sound like much, but everything I did had to be done in the same way all the time. I trapped myself in routine and sameness until eventually I never involved myself in anything that wasn't familiar to me. You can imagine how limiting that was. Finally, I was so fearful that I was afraid to leave my residence because I was sure that something outside would have changed, and I knew that I couldn't cope with any kind of change. I deluded myself into thinking that I was afraid something would happen that I couldn't control, but really it was all just an avoidance mechanism to keep me from making choices. A very sad way to live. I was as crippled as you were, Wee Bet, with your illnesses."

"Is there a common element here, Clarence?" Ho Yung has been listening thoughtfully, as we all have, and he forms the question.

"Aye. And what do you think that would be, Ho Yung?"

"I'm not exactly sure, but what we've been hearing all sounds related in some way. Even though the various manifestations differ, the results are the same. So many negative feelings and actions. So many roadblocks. So much...."

"Ego." The word falls out of my mouth before I can stop it. "I'm sorry, Ho Yung, I don't mean to interrupt you. Please, go on."

"No. No, Ardeth. I couldn't find the right word to complete my sentence, so please finish your thought."

Now everyone is looking at me. "Well, I was just thinking that everything that's been said somehow comes down to our sense of self. Fear masks our ability to see who we are. As I said before, it wears many faces. We use fear to control because we don't think we're in charge. Whether you're talking about killing people who aren't like you, or being afraid to be healthy, it all amounts to the same thing. Am I right, Clarence?"

"Aye, lassie. But this is too much conversation. We must see more to learn. Action often teaches more than talk."

Right. So right. We say our goodbyes to the couple, and I continue to walk down the Midway. I feel like I've been standing in one place too long, and it feels good to move again. The rest of the group goes on without me, but I stop a moment to listen to music I hear coming from a bandstand just ahead.

Dancing Lessons

We're always connected because we're all one.

As I walk closer to the bandstand I can see that the music is being played by a small band, all of whom are dressed in red and white striped blazers and straw hats. Red, white, and blue bunting drapes the bandstand, and hundreds of balloons are tied to the posts holding up the roof. The band is playing a jazzy dance tune, and the dance floor in front of the bandstand is crowded with people moving energetically to the beat of the music. Now this is more like it. I move in closer so I can see the dancers as well as listen to the music.

There must be at least a dozen couples out there on the dance floor, and they're really good. These aren't amateurs at all. Their ability to give visual life to music with the movement of their bodies is impressive. I really must learn to dance.

"Excuse me, Miss. Would you like to dance?"

I feel a tug on my jacket and turn to see a young boy standing behind me. He wears red pants, white shirt, and blue shoes. The face that looks up at me is covered in freckles, and

I can see a gap between two of his front teeth when he smiles. Very cute.

"I'm sorry, but I don't know how to dance."

"That's okay. I'll teach you. C'mon, it's easy."

Before I can protest he grabs my hand and leads me to the dance floor. Well, actually it's more like he's dragging me. I continue to sputter about not being able to dance, but he doesn't pay any attention to me at all. He pulls me to the center of the floor as the other dancers make room for us. He grins up at me.

"Just move to the beat of the music. Watch me and do what I do. Don't worry. You can do it."

Easy for him to say. As I watch him it becomes clear that he can dance as well as the rest of the people here, despite his young age. I do what he does, and soon my hesitant steps become more confident. Before I know it, I'm dancing with him.

"That's it. See, I knew you could do it. You don't need to watch my feet any more. Just feel the beat of the music and have fun."

Reluctantly, I take my eyes away from his feet and try to feel the music. Soon I don't have to really try because I'm moving so effortlessly I feel like a real dancer. I *am* a real dancer. Who would have thought it?

We dance several more numbers together, each dance giving me more confidence, and when the band stops to take a break,

I'm ready to stop too, but I'm energized and laughing.

My partner leads me to a bench near the side of the bandstand, and I plop happily beside him. I'm tired, but it's a good tired.

"Thank you, young man. That was really fun."

"You're welcome. You've never been here before, have you? I'm here all the time, and I've never seen you."

"No, actually this is the first time I've been to the bandstand. I don't think I even knew it was here. You're a wonderful dancer. You must enjoy dancing."

"Oh yeah, I love to dance. You do too. I can tell. You did great; you should dance more often."

"Thank you. You're a wonderful teacher, and yes, you're right; I should dance more often."

I hear the musicians begin to play again and am about to ask my new friend for another dance, but before I can frame the question I see his smile fade, and he suddenly becomes very still.

"Are you all right? Is anything wrong?"

He turns to me and shakes his head. "I'm fine. I just hear them crying, and I don't know how to help them. They don't hear me, and I can't comfort them if they won't listen. It's so frustrating."

"I'm sorry; I don't understand. Who's crying?" I look around, thinking he must be referring to someone nearby, but no one around us is crying. I only hear laughter and music.

"It's my family. They miss me, and they don't understand where I am. They don't hear me when I talk to them."

"Your family? Where are they? Why don't they hear you?"

"They're still on their visit. I left them to come Home when they thought it was too soon, and now they're grieving and I can't get through to them to console them. It's all really frustrating."

"Oh, I see now. But the grieving is necessary, don't you think?"

"Sure, but what they're doing isn't helping them at all. They keep thinking that my leaving was their fault, and they can't seem to get over it. They feel guilty, angry, and they're so sad and upset they can't seem to get on with their lives. I wish I could get through to them."

"What happens when you try?"

"Nothing. That's the problem. I can see and feel them, but they can't feel me. They don't think we're connected any more, and what's even worse, they think that just because I'm physically gone that I'm not a part of their lives any more. That's really sad. They don't get that we're always connected because we're all one. How could they not know that?"

"Did you know it when you were there?"

He looks at me in surprise. "What do you mean?"

"I'm just wondering if you knew what you know now when you were still in a body. Did you have anybody you cared about leave while you were visiting?"

"Yeah. My grandma came Home just before I did."

"Okay, then. After she left, did you still feel connected to her? Did you know where she was? Did you hear her talking to you when you were sad?"

"No. No. And, no. I felt sad because I missed her, and I didn't feel her or hear her. I know she tried to talk to me, because when she met me here, she told me so. Oh, boy. I'm expecting too much of them, aren't I?"

"Maybe. Maybe you just need to allow them to grieve for you in their own ways. I think it's a necessary process. Helps them to honor you and at the same time come to terms with the fact that you aren't physically there any longer. Maybe someday when they aren't so tied up in knots they'll hear you when you talk to them. They might be more receptive when they aren't so sad."

"I guess. I just don't like to see them this way. It wasn't their fault that I left. I made my own choice. They need to know that."

"Why? How would knowing that you chose to come Home help them now? Don't you think that if they knew that, they'd just be confused about why you wanted to leave them? Sure, it would be nice if, while we were visiting in bodies, everyone knew and understood that when somebody left they did so because of a choice they made. But you and I both know it doesn't work that way. The choice isn't usually a conscious one anyway, is it?"

"No, I guess not. You know what? We need some kind of school for dying when we're visiting. Some kind of instruction for people so they'd handle the whole experience better. This thing called death really throws people off. It's just change, but nobody gets that."

"True, but you know, I think any kind of change is hard for people. And there's always grieving involved for what is gone. It's what people do to place value on what they had. The ideal thing, I think, would be for everyone to value what they have when they have it. Then, when things change, there won't be such a sense of loss. They'll just move on. Do you see what I mean?"

"Yeah, I do."

"And so do I, but you two are missing an important point."

When I turn to see who's speaking, I see a slim woman with short blonde hair standing near us. Wire rim glasses frame intense blue eyes, and she wears the same kind of colorful outfit the dancers are wearing. Her feet move to the beat of the music as she approaches us. It's obvious from her comment that she's been listening to our conversation, but I didn't notice her until she spoke. The boy seems to know her though, and he greets her right away and invites her to sit with us on the bench.

"This is my very favorite dance partner. She's a great dancer."

The woman and I shake hands, and when I ask her to elaborate on the important point she thinks we've missed in our conversation, she's more than happy to oblige.

"Well, I was thinking that grieving is sometimes a state of mind that isn't necessarily consistent with what's real."

The look on my face must tell her that she's lost me on that one, so I give voice to my confused expression. "What does that mean? I have no idea what you just said."

She laughs and explains. "Sorry, didn't mean to be obtuse. Let me ask the young man some questions, and maybe what I mean will be clearer. When you were first told that your grandma had gone Home how did you feel?"

"Like I said before, I felt very sad."

"And would you describe this sadness as grieving?"

"Sure, that was part of it. I was kinda in shock at first because she hadn't even been sick, and I wasn't expecting her to leave. But, yeah, I was grieving."

"Okay. So you were told that your grandma had died and you immediately felt sadness, shock, and all kinds of other grieving emotions. Right?"

"Yeah. But I don't...."

"Here's my point. What if someone came to you, say several hours, or even a day after you'd been told that your grandma had died, and told you that the information was wrong because she hadn't really died. If that happened, would the new information mean that your earlier feelings of grief weren't real?"

"No, why would it? I was grieving because I thought she was gone. If somebody told me that she really wasn't gone I'd be happy, but that wouldn't change what I'd felt before. Once you have a feeling you can't just take it back."

Time to add my two cents to the discussion. "I think I see what she's saying. She's asking you to think about the fact that in her 'what if' example you were grieving about something that hadn't happened. The event wasn't real; yet, you still grieved. Isn't that what you meant by grieving being a state of mind?"

"Exactly. What we think and feel is sometimes brought on by a perceived action or event. That doesn't mean that the feeling isn't real; it's more like an emotional reaction brought about by misinformation. An illusion."

"So, if I may carry your point forward, would it not then be true that if people visiting understood that what they call death is only change, not loss – except in a physical sense – then the state of mind induced by the illusion could be understood better?" I sit back and wait for a response to what I think at that moment is a smart bit of logic.

"So right. Now we're back to little mister's idea about having a school for dying. If people understood that the death of the body makes it possible for us to return Home, then the state of mind based on their sense of permanent loss would be altered. They would still grieve for the physical loss, but knowing that their loved one had simply gone Home would make a big difference. Does that make sense?"

"Sure. It's what I was saying before about being frustrated. I want my family to know that I'm not gone from them. I want them to know that I'm still a part of them and they're still a part of me. To use your words, I guess I want them to know that their state of mind is from an illusion. The illusion of absence I guess is what I mean."

Pretty heavy stuff for a conversation that has dance music as the background. I'm about to suggest that we get up and dance again when I see Clarence walking toward us. He isn't alone though. A small gray dog, very much like the three I'd met earlier, trots along next to him. When they reach us Clarence sits down on the bench, and the dog sits on the ground in front of us.

I stare at the dog in amazement. He's glowing. Glowing! He shimmers with a light and energy that makes his small body vibrate. As I watch the pulsating light emanate from him I hear applause and cheering in the background.

The music has stopped and everyone is looking at the dog. People whistle, cheer, applaud, and laugh as he grins at them and cocks his head in a particularly charming way.

I can't resist, so I bend down and pick him up. With him sitting on my lap, I feel like I'm glowing too. It's a wonderful feeling. Joy by association.

"And who might you be, little guy?"

"Hi. My name is Cooper. How ya doin'?"

"Fine, thanks. And you're obviously very fine. Would you care to tell us what's going on here? Why are you glowing, and why is everyone applauding and cheering?"

"Well, I just got here, see. And everyone is glad to see me. That's all."

The boy reaches over to touch him and sees that his hand is glowing too. "C'mon, Cooper. There's more to it than that. What's with the glowing business?"

Cooper turns to him and gives him a quick kiss, and the boy's face starts to glow too. "I got sent Home with love. So much love that I've got enough to share. Now I can add my love to the Collective. That'll make it easier for those who didn't come Home with love. Kinda balances things out."

I remember my earlier experience with the animals in the Collective, and I instantly understand what he means. What a wonderful addition he'll be to that consciousness.

My young friend reaches over and takes Cooper on to his lap. "So, Cooper, I guess you must have had a long and happy visit with the people who gave you so much love."

"Nope. In human terms it was just a short time, couple of months is all."

"Really? So, you left your body when you were only two months old?" The boy continues to pet Cooper as they talk.

"Nope. I was about seventeen months old, but I only lived with the people who sent me Home for the last two months."

"Cooper, what do you mean when you say that the people you lived with sent you Home? Why did they do that? Were you sick?" As I ask my question, I bring him back to my lap. He's soft, and I like holding him. I also like being able to glow when he's touching me.

"Okay, you guys. Since you're so interested, here's my story. When I was about six weeks old, the breeders sold me to a family who were really mean to me. The beat me, kept food and water away from me to train me, and then they got tired of me and dumped me at one of those shelter places. Then I got adopted by an older lady who was already sad because her other dog's body was dying, and she didn't know what to do with an abused puppy. So, that didn't last long, and she brought me back to that shelter place. Then I went to stay with a really nice lady who loved me, but it was a noisy and scary house. There were three kids, another dog, a cat, and they lived in a really small place. I was scared all the time, and the lady knew that it wasn't good for me to be there. Then, my wonderful people saw a notice about me on some kind of message board or something and they called up the lady. I flew in an airplane to be with my new people, and that's where I lived until I came Home."

"Sounds like a pretty awful life until you flew away and joined your new family. But I still don't understand why they sent you Home." As I listen to him, I hold this small being in my arms and think about how very difficult it must have been for the people who loved him to let him go.

"Well, the breeders were what some folks call *backyard breeders*. They weren't responsible people, and I was born with big problems. My insides didn't work right, but nobody knew about this except me. I loved my last family so much I wanted to stay with them as long as I could, but pretty soon I couldn't eat anymore. I tried not to let on that I felt bad, but my people knew something was wrong, so they took me to a really nice animal doctor. I had some kinda tests done, and they found out that my stomach and kidneys didn't work. My people said that they loved and respected me too much to let my body starve to death, so they sent me Home with all of their love. That's why I'm glowing. I've never experienced such love, and now I get to share it."

I'm shaken by his story as are the boy and the woman. As Cooper talks, they're as close to him as I am, and I can feel their sadness. Me? I'm angry and frustrated. Here's a wonderful being that not only lived a short visit in pain and discomfort, but he'd been abused and neglected as well. Not fair. Just not fair at all. When will humans learn? Why must they continually mistreat animals?

"Ardeth, you must not allow anger to cloud your present experience with this wee laddie. He is Home now, and he is well. Be happy for that. Be in the moment with him."

"Oh, Clarence, I am. But you know, it's easier to not judge when people are dealing with people because everyone makes choices. But with animals that are subject to the choices that people make, it's so much harder not to feel anger about the way they're treated. And it's so ironic. They come to humans as messengers; they should be welcomed and loved. They should be honored and respected as teachers. Cooper, what do you think?"

"I think, Ardeth, that I'm very fortunate to have been loved so completely by my friends. They gave me a whole lifetime of love during the short time I was with them. The time before was very hard, but I'm so happy to have known the love I experienced with my family. Their love erased the past for me. And besides, I'll see them again."

The boy perks up at this comment. "You will? How do you know? Does it always work that way?"

Cooper smiles and gives me a kiss. "Oh sure. We have such a strong connection that I'll send someone with my...my essence, I guess you could say. My human friends will know that I'm a part of their new friend, and they'll welcome us into their lives again. Then we can have a longer physical time together. I really enjoyed those beach walks, rides, hugs and stuff. Got to have more of that."

Clarence stands up and motions for Cooper to join him. "Aye, laddie, that you will. But for now, the Collective waits for your energy. We must join them now."

I give Cooper one last hug and reluctantly lower him to the ground. He's still glowing, and when I look at my own body I see that I'm glowing too. I love it.

"Take care, little guy. I hope to see you again."

As Clarence and Cooper walk away, Cooper turns to me and smiles. "Oh yes, Ardeth. I'm sure we'll see each other again. Very sure."

He seems so certain. I want to ask him what he means, but in my heart I know he's right, and I really don't need to question him. I don't know how or when we'll see each other again, but I know we will. There's a connection there that's very strong. I want to tell him that I know too, but before I can speak he and Clarence have walked away.

"Wow. He said a lot, didn't he?" My dancing partner is standing now, moving to the beat of the music that had started again while we'd been talking with Cooper. "He sure knew how to enjoy the time he had with that family who really loved him, didn't he? Really says a lot about how time really isn't important. How about if we follow his lead and enjoy what we have right now. How about another dance?"

"Absolutely, my friend. Lead the way."

The woman sits on the bench while the boy and I dance. We dance, and dance, and dance, until the music stops. Finally, when my feet simply won't move any longer, I tell my new friend that it's time for me to continue on my way. We say our goodbyes and promise to keep in touch. I tell him that when I'm visiting I'll be sure to listen for him. He smiles and says all I have to do is hear the music, and I'll know he isn't far away.

THE TUNNEL OF LOVE

Sometimes it's hard to deal with what is when you've
programmed yourself to see things a different way.

I continue walking, and up ahead a big sign, somewhat faded, announces that I've almost arrived at The Tunnel of Love. Ta dah! I see the rest of my group gathered near the exit and make my way over to them.

They haven't been able to resist the popcorn either. Or the cotton candy. Dorothy has a box of popcorn in each hand, and she's trying to talk and eat at the same time. I can barely see Arturo and Consuela's faces, because they're half hidden behind huge, pink cones of cotton candy. Thomas and Louise are sharing a large pretzel loaded with mustard, and some of it is dribbling down Thomas's impeccably starched collar. I love seeing that blemish on his stuffed shirt, and I'm sure his hands are sticky too. Ice cream and candy for Wee Bet. One of each. Ho Yung has a tall, cool drink, and Clarence is eating peanuts. I definitely don't want to go. This is too much fun.

I'm on my way over to share Dorothy's popcorn when Clarence draws my attention to the exit. "Ardeth, I believe I see a friend of yours just coming out of the tunnel. She has someone waiting for her, but you might wish to speak to her too."

I look toward the exit and see that the little train and its passengers has emerged and is coming to a stop. The nurse from England is among the first to get out.

I hurry over to her and give her my hand as she steps out of the train. "Welcome Home. Did you have a pleasant journey?"

She looks just a bit bewildered, but only for a moment. When her eyes focus she recognizes me immediately. "Oh, it's you! I'm awfully glad to see you. Both of you. (Her eyes have also taken in the one who's been waiting for her.) I had a feeling you'd be here, but I wasn't sure actually. Everything seemed to happen so fast that I didn't have much time to think. I remember the explosion and then the journey through the tunnel. Before I knew it, I was coming out. And here I am."

I take her arm and begin introducing her to the rest of the group. They welcome her, and soon she's sharing what's left of Dorothy's popcorn and chattering like she's known all of them for a long time. The one who has come to meet her stands quietly by her side, his hand on her arm. A very comfortable Homecoming. Well, I guess that settles the question of resuming our previous relationship. She's Home now and won't need a guide any longer. Now she can be a guide herself if she chooses.

"Hey! Where am I? What's going on here?"

The body attached to the loud, insistent voice is charging around like a trapped animal. He's a big man. Belligerent. Confused. Pushing and shoving. Not happy at all.

"Easy, lad. Easy. Just be calm." As the man shoves his way through the group, Clarence reaches out to take his arm.

"Who are you? Get your hands off me. Get away from me!"

Clarence removes his arm, but he doesn't back off. "If you will just settle, I will be happy to tell you who I am and where you are, but I can not talk to you if you are going to shout."

The tone of voice does it. The man stops flailing and looks around him. His anger is replaced by uncertainty, and he looks as though he might collapse.

"Here. Come and sit down. You'll feel better in a minute." Wee Bet takes his arm and leads him to a bench near the ticket booth. "Now, just sit quietly, and you'll be fine."

"But…but…what is this place? Where am I? Who are all of you people? I don't understand. Am I dead? It isn't supposed to be like this. I wasn't ready yet, and I don't know why I'm here. I want to go home."

"You are Home, laddie. We will talk, and you will understand soon enough. When you feel up to it, we will walk a bit."

Quite a different Homecoming for this one. All depends on your point of view I guess. And what you expect. After he and Clarence have a talk, he'll feel better. Sometimes it's hard to deal with what is when you've programmed yourself to see things a different way. Another lesson to be learned.

I'm about ready to continue on my way when I hear someone laughing. When I turn to see where the sound is coming from, I see a man coming out of the tunnel. He's smiling, laughing, and is one very happy guy. I'm too curious to just keep walking, so I go over to him. He's being met by a small boy, but they both stop and turn to me.

"Excuse me. I'm sorry to interrupt your Homecoming, but I heard your laughter, and I can't help but wonder what you've experienced that's left you in such a happy frame of mind."

"Oh, hi there. You aren't interrupting. My boy and I were just going to meet some other people, but we'd be glad to stop and talk. What do you need to know?"

"Well, I'm just wondering why you're so happy, that's all."

"Oh, I see. I guess I could tell you, but maybe it'd be more interesting if you saw for yourself. Have you been to the Chamber of Joy?"

"No, I haven't. Where is it?"

"Which direction are you going?"

"Right now, I'm just walking down the Midway. Eventually, I'll get to the Chute. Why?"

He turns me around and points to a large building not far away. "See that building over there? Go on over and check it out. You'll find the Chamber of Joy inside, and you'll get your answer. Nice seeing you."

Before I can ask anything else, the man and boy continue on their way. I'm looking at the building he indicated, but I need to get closer to see what it is. All I can see from this distance is a big face over the doorway. Wouldn't hurt to take a little detour.

THE CHAMBER OF JOY

Just be still; listen to your heart.

When I approach the building I can see that the face over the entrance is a clown face. It's one of those faces that has a big red nose and a huge smiling mouth. Big eyes. Frizzy white hair sticks out from under a funny looking hat. Above the clown face are the words "Fun House." Okay, I guess that makes sense. The laughing man wants me to go into the Fun House. Why not? Seems like a logical place to find the Chamber of Joy.

I open the door and enter the building. As soon as I'm inside I'm met by myself. The walls of the room are covered with mirrors and my image, distorted in a hundred different ways, looks back at me. The sight is disconcerting to say the least. When I move, the mirror images move. Some are long and skinny. Others are fat and short. They all look like me, but I'm seeing distorted versions of myself that are very strange indeed.

"Pretty neat, isn't it?"

I turn around and come face to face with someone I've met before. It's the basketball player from the meadow. He still has the basketball in his hands, but now he's just holding it and smiling at me.

I smile back and greet him. "Hello. I remember you from the meadow. Are you part of another one of Clarence's set-ups? Is he around somewhere?"

"No, actually I'm the tour guide for this attraction. And, Clarence isn't here, as far as I can tell. Do you want to go on the tour or are you looking for something in particular?"

"Well, actually I'm looking for the Chamber of Joy, but I'd like to go on the tour too as long as I'm here. When we met in the meadow you said that you were practicing so you could learn to have fun. Is that why you're in the Fun House?"

He smiles and starts to bounce the ball. His mirror images bounce too; he's become a whole team of basketball players. Interesting effect. "Well, not really. I'm getting ready to go on a visit too, and this is a great place to get in the mood for what I have in mind. C'mon. I'll give you the whole tour; that way you can see what all is here, including the Chamber of Joy."

I follow the basketball man to the far end of the room. We're approaching a section of the mirrored wall that makes both of us look like short, squatty creatures with pushed in faces. Not very flattering. I wait as he touches the lower right hand corner of the mirrored panel directly in front of us, and I hear a clicking noise as the panel opens. He walks through the opening and I follow. Alice in Wonderland at the Fun House.

The room we enter is like a movie theater. Well, I guess it is a movie theater. There are plush seats facing a large screen that's set up at the front of the room. Quite a few people are seated, and some of them are even eating popcorn. My guide leads us to two seats near the front of the room. We're so close to the screen I have to look up a bit to see it.

"Tell me what you see, Ardeth."

"I see a large screen. Nothing's happening right now so I guess the show hasn't started yet. What movie are we going to watch? I'll bet it's a comedy, considering where we are."

"Look down at the arm-rest on your seat. Do you see the red button?"

"Yes, I see it. Am I supposed to push it to make the movie start?"

"That's right. If you look closely, you'll see a little sign above the button.

Sure enough. Right above the button is a label that reads "Preview of Coming Attractions." I push the button and immediately the room is filled with the sound of trumpets. The lights dim, and as the fanfare reaches a finale the screen lights up to reveal a panoramic view of the solar system. As I watch, the planets, stars, everything I can see on the screen begin to move in a swirling effect of light. I'm swept away by the visual effects, and the orchestra music that accompanies the movement on screen is irresistible. My foot starts to tap, and I can feel myself smiling. This is really wonderful.

I'm lost, and I love it. I have no sense of my immediate surroundings at all anymore. I'm just aware of the images on the screen and the music. Nothing else is relevant or important. As the images continue to move, I can feel myself getting out of my seat. I don't have a conscious sense of direction, but I'm walking toward the screen. I only know that I want to be there – wherever *there* is – and I want to be there right now. As I walk forward, my eyes never leave the screen. Somehow I manage to get to the screen without stumbling, and without really being aware of why or how I just walk right through the screen. It's as if the screen just dissolves around me.

Now I'm in another room. I look around disappointed because I somehow had hoped that I'd be out there in the universe somewhere, along with the planets, stars, and whatever else is out there. But here I am in an ordinary room.

"Disappointed, aren't you?"

I turn and see that the basketball man has joined me and clearly has read my thoughts. "Yes, I am. What happened to the solar system? That's where I thought I was going. How do I get there?"

Basketball man smiles and shakes his head. "You are there, Ardeth. What you saw on the screen was just a preview of coming attractions. Just a glimpse of all that's available to you. Look around you. This room is more interesting than you think."

He's right. At first I thought this was just a room with walls, but now I can see that this is really a room with many doors. In fact, there are several doors set in each wall. Each door is painted a different color, and above each door is a symbol. I don't know what the symbols mean, but some of them look like stars. Others depict trees, water, buildings, just a whole array of pictures, some of which remind me of images that I saw on the screen. Aha! I get it. The big screen preview has narrowed to a smaller picture that might allow me to experience many places. Each door probably opens into a different location. Very clever.

"Go on. Check out the doors. Open them and see what you find." My guide starts to bounce the ever present basketball as he watches me.

I'm not sure which door to open first, so I just begin with the one directly in front of me. It's a blue door, and when I open it I see a huge body of water. Dolphins and all kinds of sea creatures are swimming lazily in front of me. It's very inviting, and I'm tempted to join them, but I'm too curious about the other doors to do that just yet. Maybe later.

I choose another door, this one green, and I'm treated to the sight of children playing in a park. They're laughing and having a wonderful time. Okay, that's good. What's next?

This is really fun. I quickly move from door to door, opening each one, eager to see what lies beyond the threshold. Each scene is different, but there's a common element to all of them. Whether I find myself looking at people just walking together or seeing a forest with slants of sunlight illuminating the trees, every scene is happy, peaceful, and there's a sense of joy in all of them.

"Am I in the Chamber of Joy now? Is that what this is all about?" I've opened and closed all of the doors now, and I'm back in the center of the room with Basketball Man.

"Nope. But we're getting close. What do you think about what you saw behind the doors?"

"I like what I saw. All of the scenes were happy and peaceful. Very nice. There were quite a few that I'd like to visit."

"So, what do you think they all mean? What's the message?"

"I'm not sure. I think there's a big message to this whole experience of being in the Fun House, but I'm not ready to say yet. I'd still like to see the Chamber of Joy, since that's why I'm here. May we go there now?"

"Sure. Here's how you get there. Just close your eyes and think about five things that make life possible. Five things that are intrinsic to life. Visualize them. When you see them in your mind, say them out loud so I can hear you."

"Five things essential for life? Interesting question. Is this some kind of quiz? Is there a right answer?"

Basketball Man laughs. "Well, Ardeth, I suppose it's a quiz, but really it's more a test of your awareness. Here's the way it works. I'm talking about the laws of the universe here, and when you name them, you'll find yourself in the Chamber of Joy."

More and more interesting. "Okay, I need to think about this. I've never thought about the laws of the universe before."

"Don't think, Ardeth. Just be still; listen to your heart, and see what comes to you."

My mind is going in all directions, and it's hard to empty it and be still, but I try because somehow I know this is important. I quiet my breathing and focus on just listening to the beating of my heart. At first nothing, and then I can hear it. The sound is comforting and almost hypnotic. Now I'm quiet. I see…a heart, a dove, swirling colors, a candle, and a hand reaching out. As I see the images I say the first words that come to mind.

"Love. Peace. Imagination. Discovery. Thank you."

As soon as the words have been said, I find myself in another room, but this room is very different from the previous rooms. No mirrors or doors. Just a space without walls that's filled with an intense energy that's almost palpable. The symbols that I saw before I said the words are all here, moving with the same ballet movement that I saw in the solar system.

"Open your arms, Ardeth. Welcome joy. Welcome life."

I do, and I'm filled with an overwhelming sense of happiness. The words I said are inside of me, giving me energy and a sense of contentment that makes me feel complete. I don't really understand the why and how of what's going on, but it doesn't matter. I feel joy.

Suddenly there's a shift of some kind, and I find myself back out on the Midway standing near the Tunnel of Love. I don't know how I got back here, but I look around and see Clarence standing by my side. He's smiling. Naturally.

"Well, lassie. Have you had an interesting adventure that you wish to discuss?"

"Interesting? That seems like an understatement, Clarence. And I definitely want to talk about what I've just experienced. What was that all about?"

"What do you think, lassie? Certainly, you must have some notion in your mind."

"Well, actually I have all sorts of ideas, but I don't know which ones are relevant. I loved the whole experience, but I'm not sure why the laughing man wanted me to go there. How does what I saw and felt explain why he was so happy? No, let me say that differently. I can understand why the Chamber of Joy would cause someone to feel happy, but how does it relate to why he was happy? He'd just returned from a visit, and I don't think the visit was to the Chamber of Joy. That's here, and the visit was somewhere else. Wasn't it?"

"Aye, lass. His visit was to another place. Allow me to ask a question. Why does one go on a visit?"

"Why? To learn, of course. Each visit gives us an opportunity to learn the lessons we assign ourselves."

"Just so. And are all of these lessons serious and difficult?"

"Well, not always I suppose. Some lessons are more difficult than others. Depends on what they are. I'm not sure that I get your point."

"My point, as you say, Ardeth, is that visits are not always serious journeys. Some can be just for fun. To experience joy. The laughing man, as you call him, had just returned from a joyful visit, and he wanted you to know that the same choice is available to you. That is why he sent you to the Chamber of Joy. That is why the lad you met in the meadow was there, preparing himself for his next visit. If you carry with you the five concepts you thought of in the Chamber, you will better understand how to make your visit joyful. Do you see?"

"Are you telling me that I should make my next visit one in which I just experience joy and have fun? Is that what you're saying?"

"I am not telling you that you should do one thing or another, lass. I am simply saying that visits can be fun. There are times when people lose sight of that option. That is all I am saying."

"Okay, I understand. But tell me, please, about the five things intrinsic to life that I came up with in the Chamber."

"What is it you wish to know?"

"I'd just like you to comment on each of them and maybe explain why they're so important. That's all."

"Aye. Let us take love, first. Love and the sense of oneness it generates frees you to encompass all. What you draw to you in love is compatible with you and allows you to experience joy. Peace is self-explanatory is it not? But I must say that in seeking peace you must not ignore stress, which is part of the continuum. Stress provides you with the impetus to change. Then there is imagination. This is the quality that allows you to discover the potential in all things. That is discovery. And finally, there is thank-you. What is not clear about that idea, lass?"

"What's not clear is who I'm thanking, Clarence. To whom am I saying *thank-you*?"

"Why, to yourself, of course, Ardeth. When you thank yourself, that thought creates a ripple effect out from you, and the ripples cause others to do the same. And so on. Do you see?"

"Yes, I do. So, you're saying that those five things are not only intrinsic to life itself, but they create a joyful life. Is that right?"

"Aye, lass. Just so. No more discussion now. I will leave you to your thoughts."

Leave me to my thoughts. Right. I have enough of those to last several lifetimes. While I'm thinking, I watch a few more individual homecomings and am about to continue on my way when I see a flurry of movement at the group exit of the Tunnel. This particular exit is reserved for large groups of people who return Home at the same time, and right now a huge crowd is emerging. I walk over for a closer look.

GROUP HOMECOMINGS

The individual is contained in the whole, and the whole is contained in the individual.

More people than I can begin to count walk out of the exit. Most of them appear to be bewildered and confused, clearly not realizing yet where they are. Men, women, and children pour from the Tunnel. As I watch from a distance, many look around and begin to smile. Others shake their heads, trying to make sense of what is happening. Amazingly enough, there seems to be at least one person or animal greeting each of the newcomers. Those who have come to welcome speak their greetings, and each new arrival is gently led off by his or her greeter. Remarkable that this can happen so effortlessly in exactly the same way that it did when the individuals we'd just seen had emerged. It doesn't seem to matter that there are thousands arriving. The same process occurs.

"Do you have a question about what you are seeing, Ardeth?" Clarence is standing next to me with his hand on my arm.

"Yes. No. Well, not really a question about what I'm seeing now. I know that regardless of how many come Home, there will always be those who come to greet them. I guess my question has to do with how it happens that so many choose to come Home at the same time. How does that work? I've never been part of a group departure before, so I have no experience to guide me in understanding."

"Lassie, it is no different than when an individual comes Home. Why is this difficult to understand?"

"Well, I suppose it's hard to grasp because of the numbers involved. What we're seeing here are thousands of people who've chosen to end their visits at exactly the same time. Many, or perhaps most of them, don't even know each other. This has happened many times in history, I know, but I've never understood how it could be."

"All right, lass, let me ask you this question. Do you understand that we are all one?"

"Yes, Clarence, we've talked about this many times. I know that we're all one."

"Aye. And because we are all one, we are all connected. Is that not so?"

"Yes, of course. But...."

"And, if we are all connected, we are part of what you might call a group consciousness. Just as the animals you met earlier. We are all one spirit, if you will. This group consciousness is like a hologram. Do you know what that is, lassie?"

"Yes, Clarence. I'm familiar with holograms, but what does that have to do with my question?"

"Your question has everything to do with holograms if you understand the concept, Ardeth. Let me show you. Look again at the group leaving the tunnel. Tell me what you see."

I do as instructed, and what I see is fascinating. Well, no, it's actually more than that. The people emerging are frozen, for just one photographic moment, in a large holographic image. Their auras shimmer, and the colors all blend together in a vivid patchwork of beings. Then, as I continue to watch, individuals move away from the group image, but I can still see the whole picture in each specific image. Now I'm confused. What am I seeing?

"I observe that you do not quite grasp what you are seeing, Ardeth. Allow me to explain the principle of a holograph. When you remove a portion of the whole image, just as you are seeing now as individuals walk away from the group picture, that fragment still contains the whole image. And, if you were to remove a section from the image you have just taken away, the whole would still be contained in that piece. No matter how small the segment, the whole image still remains."

"So, then, are you saying that all life forms are part of some gigantic holographic energy? And that, maybe, the entire universe is the big picture, so to speak? Is that what you're saying?"

"Aye, lass. That is exactly what I am saying."

"Well, I think I understand the theory, but I still don't see how that answers my question. What you've just shown me explains the 'we are all one' concept very nicely, but it doesn't answer why so many people choose to come Home at the same moment in time. I know. I know. There isn't any time, but you know what I mean."

"Aye. Perhaps a different kind of explanation is in order. Allow me another question, if you please. Is there any difference between what you might call the common cold and the illness referred to as pneumonia?"

"Well, sure. A cold isn't as serious as pneumonia. Many people develop colds, but not nearly as many suffer from pneumonia."

"But is the principle the same, Ardeth? Are they not both illnesses?"

"Yes, but...."

"But what? Are they not simply symptoms that exist at different ends of a continuum? When you say that a cold isn't as serious as pneumonia, you are making a judgment. They are both illnesses manifested by the thoughts of those who exhibit the symptoms. There is no difference. Just as there is no difference between the death of one individual and the deaths of many. The same principle exists in both cases. The individual is contained in the whole, and the whole is contained in the individual. You are too concerned with numbers and values here. When many choose to come Home at what you would call the same time, you are just viewing a different end of the continuum than you would be if you only viewed the departure of one. The principle is the same. The degree does not make a difference."

My head is spinning. Just when I think I have a grasp of what he's saying, comprehension slips away from me before I can embrace it and call it understanding. I'm missing something important. I don't get the connection. Connection. That's it.

"Clarence, what do all of these people we see arriving at the same time have in common? I understand that they're all connected, in a holographic sense, but why did they all choose to be in the same place at the same time? Was there some kind of agreement among them – at least on a psychic level – that they would all leave together? Is that it?"

"Now, you approach the concept of vibrational frequency, lass. And, that is certainly one way to understand what we are discussing. Aye, those who choose to leave together, because of the circumstances in which they place themselves, all share similar vibrational frequencies. They are drawn together, many times not in any conscious way, and that coming together affords them the opportunity to leave together, if they choose. All life is an experience, and those who choose a group departure desire to have a group experience."

"But in a mass leaving those who arrive Home as a result of whatever brought about the deaths of their bodies certainly didn't cause the instrument of their departure, did they?

They had no choice about that."

"Nay, lass. But they all did choose to be together, knowing that the situation in which they found themselves might afford them the opportunity to leave. Their knowing was not conscious, but they did know just the same."

"How could they know? What happens on a subconscious level to make that kind of knowing possible?

"The level that you refer to as being subconscious is really more appropriately termed as the level of connectedness, if I may use such a term. Regardless of where you choose to visit, a part of you always remains at Home. And that part...."

"Wait just a moment, Clarence. I'm sorry to interrupt, but I need some clarification here. Is that part of us that remains at Home our soul? Or is it our spirit?"

"Call it what you will, lassie. You are dealing in semantics here, and it is not necessary. Just know that a part of you remains at Home. Always. And you are always connected to that part of you. And, in fact, when you return Home, you become one with yourself. You are then complete."

"So, if I understand you correctly, when we visit other places we are always connected to that part of us at Home. It sounds a bit like some kind of psychic umbilical cord. That's a really comforting thought. I like that idea very much. It makes sense to me. And, with that understanding, everything else you've said falls into place too. Very neat."

"Aye, lass. You are learning more and more. That is very good. There is just one more thought I wish for you to consider within the context of our conversation. Think of what a group departure teaches others."

"Others? Do you mean those who are left behind, so to speak, when a group departure occurs?"

"Aye, lassie. Think of the impact on a society when many leave their bodies. Think of the opportunity to learn for those who witness or learn about a group departure. Often, as a result of what some would call a tragedy, valuable lessons are learned by others. Those lessons are often gifts given by those who choose to leave; gifts that perhaps would not be accepted in any other way. The poet John Donne wrote that the deaths of others diminished him because he was a part of all mankind, but he was too busy grieving to learn. What people call death, regardless of whether it is a single passing or a group exodus, should not diminish others. Those who have lessons yet to learn can be made more complete, not diminished, by the leaving of others if they resolve to learn what the passing of others can teach them if they are willing to learn. Do you see this, lass?"

"I do see, Clarence, but before we move on I need to ask you a question that came up for me when we were in your office. My question relates to the connectedness we've been talking about, but it also speaks to some confusion on my part."

"Aye, lass. Go on. Why are you confused?"

"I'm confused because I know that when we're Home we have a broader understanding of who we are and our relationships with various people. I know, for instance, that Ho Yung, Wee Bet and I know each other and have shared lives together. Why didn't I remember that when I saw them? All I got were brief glimpses of our various times together. And, all of the lessons I've been learning as we walked down the lane and those I've learned here in the Park are lessons I should already have learned because I'm Home. Why am I being so limited here? When we're Home there are no limits."

"Ardeth, allow me to ask you this. Why did you come to my office, and why have you walked down the lane to the Park?"

"I came by your office to ask if I could use your name in the book I want to write, and I walked down the lane to the Park because I'm about to leave on a visit."

"Aye, just so. You are in what might perhaps be called a transitional phase of being Home. You are preparing for your journey, and part of that preparation involves focusing on what is about to become real for you, rather than experiencing all of you and your various connections to other people. You are narrowing your vision to accommodate what you will be learning on your visit. You will bring what you know of Home and your awareness here with you, but that awareness and the lessons you have learned here will not be, as you might say, conscious realizations for you. Do you understand, lass?"

"I do, now that you explain it this way, but it just seems as though I should have been more aware here than I have been. It's very frustrating to feel that you know something, but then to realize that you don't know as much as you think you do."

Clarence smiles and winks at me as he takes my arm. "But lass, think upon this. If the many adventures we have shared together, as well as those you have shared with others, are so clearly drawn in your mind, what then do you have to offer in the way of lessons and how they are learned as you write your book?"

Aha! Now it all makes sense. I get it. "Okay, Clarence, one last question. May I use your name in the book?"

"Of course, lassie. You already are."

And so I am. Oh, my...so much to learn.

Speaking of learning, I really do have to be on my way. I can see the Chute just up ahead at the end of the Midway, and I start toward it. Slowly. Ever so slowly.

My friends follow me silently. They know how I feel. Nobody says anything, but I think we've all run out of words. Besides, love doesn't always need words to find a heart.

THE CHUTE

It's time. Get on with it.

As I walk toward the Chute – a multicolored tubular rainbow shining in the sun – the noises of the Park seem to fade a bit. It's just me; I know that. But all the same, I want to reach out and hang on to the comfort of familiar sounds and smells. Fields of mustard. Flowers. Friends.

A few more steps. When I reach the stairs, I pause and turn around. They're all there. Ho Yung. Arturo, Consuela. Louise. Thomas. Wee Bet. And Dorothy. All a part of me. I smile tentatively and throw the teddy bear I won earlier to Ho Yung. I've been carrying my prize ever since the little boy gave it to me, but I don't need the stuffed bear now. At some point in my childhood I'm sure someone will give me another one. As Ho Yung catches the bear he smiles back at me, and his face changes to one I don't recognize. Yet.

Clarence? Where is he? For a moment I think he isn't with the group, but then I see him standing just a little bit behind the others. He's smiling that smile again. I can almost hear him.

195

"Go ahead, lassie. You will be fine. We will not be far away."

I begin to climb the stairs. With each step my feet grow heavier, and I have to literally pull myself up the last few steps to the platform. Good thing there's a railing here.

When I get to the top, I turn for a final look. It isn't such a long climb, but my friends all look very small and far away. I can barely hear the noises of the Park now. Very faint. The giant wheel is still spinning, and in the distance I think I can see a dim haze of yellow. I wonder if the fields will still be there when I return. Or, perhaps I might see the ocean next time.

All right, Ardeth. No more stalling. Headache or not, it's time. Get on with it.

I turn and face the opening of the Chute. Maybe it won't take so long this time. If I can just get there without all of that banging around. I bend down and crawl inside, careful not to lose my balance. It's a bit like sitting in an enclosed sled. I know I can't sit here forever, yet I hesitate as I'm about to shove off because once I get started it's really hard to stop. I hang on to the top of the Chute, trying to find a comfortable position, but there isn't any. Looking down the Chute I think I see a very faint light in the distance, but it's probably just wishful thinking. Actually, it's dark. Very dark. I wait just a moment longer, trying to collect my thoughts. A deep breath, and then....

Down I go. Slowly at first, and then faster and faster. Another bumpy ride. My head starts to pound. Here we go again.

Chicago, here I come.

EPILOGUE

My stay in Chicago lasted only a few years in measured time, just long enough to become a daughter to the two people who had been so faithful to me when I visited the Canary Islands. On this visit I watched over them as best I could until our lives took us from Illinois to Michigan to California. They returned Home shortly after the move to California.

Once in California, I met Ho Yung again and we became partners. Dorothy joined Ho Yung in establishing a florist and nursery business, and we soon met Arturo and Consuela, who had found each other again after her stay in England, and his in Minnesota. We all reconnected with Louise and Thomas. Dorothy, Thomas, Louise, and Arturo have returned Home again. Wee Bet lives in Tennessee, but she writes from time to time and came to visit when we were in California. She married the balloonist we met when we were in that space between.

Did I remember all of them when we met again? No, but Clarence helped us re-establish our connection to each other.

Do they have the same names, personalities and gender that distinguished them when they were in that space between? Their names have changed, and with some, including Ho Yung, the gender has changed also. Some aspects of their personalities remain, as do mine.

Tuppence, Duncan and Duffy joined Ho Yung and me in California as our first animal family. They were followed by many others: Henry, Molly, Fitz, Pip, Jenny, Joey, Angus, Cooper, Harper, Teddy, Josie, MacTavish, and Sammy.

After living many years in California, Ho Yung and I moved to Washington with our animal family. New and old friends joined us, and Clarence was a regular visitor to our home. He always comes when he is called, and he is with us in our dreams. We have lived our lives in love and abundance, learning our lessons, enjoying the visit.

Five years ago – in illusion time – after forty earth years as my loving partner, Ho Yung returned Home to contemplate his lessons and prepare for his next expression of spirit. I will join him when my lessons are complete…for this visit.

At this moment, however, I'm still learning how to live my life according to the laws of the universe:

> *Love*
> *Peace*
> *Imagination*
> *Discovery*
> *Thank you*

I wish you joy.

www.ingramcontent.com/pod-product-compliance
Lightning Source LLC
Chambersburg PA
CBHW051957090426
42741CB00008B/1429